Real Words from

"Thank you for being such an honest and true voice for so many moms out there."
—Jen K.

"You help me get through the days when I am not sure what I have gotten myself into and when I question if I am cut out for motherhood. Thank you."
—Heather B.

"Thank you for allowing me to see the truth that has been staring me in the face and for giving me the strength to move forward with what is best for my children and me."
—T.E.

"Your writing helps me feel less alone and often gives me the little boost I need to dig deep and keep going."
—Jenifer J.

"Thank you so much for showing me that I'm normal, that mothering my children is an imperfect science of trial and error, and that it's okay not to be perfect. Thank you."
—Heather W.

"Today you bring tears to my eyes. You make me feel like somebody gets it. Somebody understands."
—Becky R.

"The wisdom you share is life changing and gives me hope in the days when I need it the most."

—Kristi B.

"When I read your honest reflections, I hear an assuring voice whisper back, 'You are not alone.' Suddenly, my hope is renewed, and I'm able to go back to what I do best: loving my people. You have an extraordinary gift for putting into words what it means to accept and embrace the messy, hard, beautiful, sacred moments of motherhood."

—Rachel M. S.

"I am constantly riding the roller coaster that is motherhood. Thank you for your compassionate and enlightening words of strength, wisdom, and inspiration."

—Tash M.

"Your words have spoken straight to my heart. There have been times when they've been my primary encouragement."

—Jessi H.

"Sometimes your words are what keep me going when I've hit the wall of patience, energy, and self-confidence."

—Kathy S.

THE
BRAVE
ART OF MOTHERHOOD

THE
BRAVE
ART OF MOTHERHOOD

FIGHT FEAR, GAIN CONFIDENCE,
AND FIND YOURSELF AGAIN

RACHEL MARIE MARTIN
FINDINGJOY.NET

WATERBROOK

THE BRAVE ART OF MOTHERHOOD

Details in some anecdotes and stories have been changed to protect the identities of the persons involved.

Trade Paperback ISBN 978-0-7352-9139-3
eBook ISBN 978-0-7352-9140-9

Cover design by Kelly L. Howard

Published in the United States by WaterBrook, an imprint of the Crown Publishing Group, a division of Penguin Random House LLC, New York.

WATERBROOK and its deer colophon are registered trademarks of Penguin Random House LLC.

Library of Congress Cataloging-in-Publication Data
Names: Martin, Rachel Marie, author.
Title: The brave art of motherhood : fight fear, gain confidence, and find yourself again / Rachel Marie Martin.
Description: First Edition. | Colorado Springs : WaterBrook, 2018.
Identifiers: LCCN 2018012716| ISBN 9780735291393 (pbk.) | ISBN 9780735291409 (electronic)
Subjects: LCSH: Mothers—Religious life. | Motherhood—Religious aspects—Christianity.
Classification: LCC BV4529.18 .M363 2018 | DDC 248.8/431—dc23
LC record available at https://lccn.loc.gov/2018012716

Printed in the United States of America
2018—First Edition

10 9 8 7 6 5 4 3 2 1

SPECIAL SALES
Most WaterBrook books are available at special quantity discounts when purchased in bulk by corporations, organizations, and special-interest groups. Custom imprinting or excerpting can also be done to fit special needs. For information, please email specialmarketscms@penguinrandomhouse.com or call 1-800-603-7051.

For my parents

Contents

The Guide

Over the past five years, I've lived what I've jokingly called a public private life. As you'll read in this book, living the private spaces of my life in a public forum was antithetical to the "me" of most of my life. But going through great changes and having others see and read about the progress has resulted in some very common questions:

- How in the world did you change your life?
- What steps did you take?
- How did you manage change and being a mom?
- How did you discover happiness?
- Where did you get the bravery?

As a result, in the book process, I've spent a good year examining my past seven years. I didn't let any nuance sit by the wayside but rather dug deep into the details—the emotions, results, choices, and mindsets that led to me reclaiming my life. I mapped my world—the inner and outer struggles as well as the times of failing and success. Those details?

That's what this book is about.

But I need you to know from the start that this book is not a linear, chronological story of my progression from poverty to my life today. Instead, it is about the mental determination, the process, the challenges, and the how behind great change.

It's your guide and the answers to those common questions.

You will discover the agreements you've made about yourself, the excuses you give, and why your reality is what it is. But it doesn't have to be what it is. If you dare, if you decide to walk this path, to disrupt patterns that keep you stuck, all while in the midst of motherhood, I can guarantee you that your future will be different.

That is the brave art of motherhood.

Part 1

STUCK IN THE GREAT TENSION

"Be brave," says my spirit.
"Wait," says fear.
"Have courage," says my soul.
"Not yet," says worry.
"Dare," says my heart.

—Rachel Marie Martin

Dear Brave Warriors Journeying Life with Me,

Last year I was in Washington, DC, standing in the front of a room, holding a mic, speaking to a roomful of moms. As I gazed around the room at all the women looking for a word of hope, at all the moms pushing little ones in strollers in the back, at the women daring to dream, I decided to veer from my set script and tell them what was on my heart.

I shared a story of a mom who had seven kids and had the IRS knocking on her door. This mom had less than fifteen dollars in her checking account, but she also had a dream, a target of change, and an old netbook computer her parents had given her for Christmas.

I told those moms how she started to write, to dare to be real, and to spread a bit of hope. I spoke about how she suffered through a divorce and lost everything, yet in the losing, she found herself again. I explained how she got knocked down and how she stood back up, over and over.

I shared how she found happiness again.

I shared how she made a new agreement about worth.

And then I introduced that room of moms to the mom of my story.

Me.

Tears fell freely that afternoon. But they weren't tears of sadness; they were tears of hope. I took a risk to voice my story and found a bond with a roomful of women who also wanted the realness of hope. It started as a ripple and began to rush from woman to woman. We all got it; we all knew our fight; we knew we weren't alone. The more I shared, the stronger the rush of hope spread.

I knew that was why I told my story and why I'm sharing it here.

My story has worth.

Yours does too.

Embrace your story. Share it with others.

And cling to the hope that comes out of it.

                                                        —Rachel

1

Time Keeps On Ticking

I grew up in the eighties. My kids think it's epic how I lived during the generation they now deem retro. In fact, several years ago I flew cross-country to Seattle to visit my oldest daughter, Hannah, who was a sophomore in college. We hung out in her trendy local bakery, and as we ate crumbly gluten-free pastries topped with dollops of fresh whipped cream and sipped our overpriced espressos, she asked, "Hey, Mom, do you want to go to this cool vintage shop with me? I know you'll love it."

I didn't hesitate to say yes. I pushed my chair back and grabbed my coffee, and together we walked across the leaf-covered street to Hannah's favorite store, while she rapidly talked about how much I would adore this place and all the amazing objects inside.

As we wandered around the dusty shop, I observed something unexpected. In fact, I started to laugh as the reality became clearer. You see, her "vintage" store with collectible items that withstood time was not filled with the antiques I was expecting but was, in fact, filled with relics from my own childhood.

I was now vintage.

I spotted orange and lime-green Tupperware, the same as my mother once sold. Fisher-Price toys, the same ones I used to play with, now fetched a premium price. Cabbage Patch Kids, Atari game consoles, and other games I thought had disappeared lined the shelves. A wall of posters of artists I loved hung by bins of vinyl records, cassette tapes, and CDs. I flipped through them, past Huey Lewis and the News and Tears for Fears, and then saw one of my favorite tapes by the Steve Miller Band tucked in a stack. As I looked at the cover, the now poignant lyrics filled my mind: "Time keeps on slippin', slippin', slippin' into the future."[1]

While I hummed the melody, I looked up at Hannah meandering through rows of my childhood now for sale. She was looking at neon shirts, and as she thumbed through the rack, her face scrunched up just a bit. I'd seen that face before. It was long, long ago on the hot summer night when she was born. Her tiny six-pound-thirteen-ounce self came into this world with that same scrunchy face. She was a feisty newborn, completely dependent on me, her rookie mom.

I sighed heavily—the type of sigh reserved just for moms—and as she decided which eighties shirt was the best I wondered, *Where in the world did the time go?*

She didn't know I stared at her, but there she was, just a couple of years younger than I was when I'd first held her.

I remember that me. I was feisty, full of dreams, full of hopes.

Now there I stood, twenty years later, a divorced mom of seven kids, watching her and, in a way, watching myself. That sigh wasn't just about how quickly she grew up, but it was also because of the clear image of my own passage of time.

There is an unspoken tension in life. When we are young, we're oblivious to it, unaware of the movement of time. But the older we get, the more we become aware of its constant ticking.

Then one day in the middle of our life's moving timeline, we become mothers, and that timeline that was once ours alone we now share.

As moms, our time is fragmented, and we focus on our children. We stop documenting our own accomplishments and instead document theirs: a week old, a month old, a birthday, the start of school, the move to middle school, prom, graduation.

With each new milestone, we have more to do, more to keep up with, more expectations to manage. And time keeps moving, keeps ticking by. It doesn't slow down for hard times or for blissful moments or for times when we just need a break. Yet I cried when my Hannah turned one, because I felt as though I'd already lost a year of her childhood due to time's tick.

"Slow down, time, slow down," I'd pleaded.

But life gets busy, so busy that the appreciation of time's movement gradually shifts to those days when we quietly chant under our breath, "I just want to make it through." There are times when we can't wait for the day to end, when the burdens and expectations keep piling up and there doesn't seem to be enough of us to go around. There are days of slammed doors, cranky kids, and "I hate you! You're the worst mom ever!" when we're just trying to be the "good" mom. Next thing we know, we're another mom in a march of moms who are going through the motions of motherhood, joking about the moments of peace we *might* get at the end of the day, cursing the homework our kids whine about, and telling one another we'll join that kickboxing class when our schedules get less busy.

We become so focused on getting through motherhood and doing for our kids that somehow we lose sight of all the mothering our mothers did during our own childhoods. Think of all the piano lessons, recitals, and orchestra concerts our moms went to for us. The soccer practices and cheerleading competitions. The constant shuttling to and from our high school jobs. They spent their precious time helping us grow and achieve our goals and skills and loves.

The world was at our feet, and our moms helped and encouraged us to discover our passions. Yet when we become mothers, the focus of priorities shifts. Instead of continuing to pursue our dreams, we abandon them and copy what our moms did before us. We put ourselves on the back burner to help our children achieve *their* dreams, knowing the whole time that we're only helping them achieve the dreams they have before they, too, become parents.

What if you broke that cycle in your family? What if you decided to teach your children that those skills and dreams you fostered as a child are just as important for improving your entire life, and in so doing, you take moments out of your schedule to focus on you? I'm not suggesting that you no longer help your kids achieve their dreams; I'm suggesting that you do it *alongside* continuing to pursue yours. What if seeing you do that means that they, too, will pursue their dreams their entire lives?

Just as Steve Miller sang, "Time keeps on slippin'," we don't have unending amounts of time to someday get back to doing what we dreamed of. Every tick of the clock is a minute further in our lives. When I first held Hannah in my arms, I felt as if I had an infinite number of ticks. Twenty-one years of the clock flipping over and over have since happened. And when I stood in that Seattle vintage store, I realized that the art of life, of motherhood, happens when we exhale and cherish today *while* we also seize the moment, the inch of time today, and move ourselves forward to reclaim who we are meant to be.

For so many years I went through the motions. I got busy with motherhood, learned to accept reality as unchangeable, and existed. I didn't have a fire to appreciate that inch of today. Instead, I took it for granted. You probably do that too.

At a certain point, the inches will run out. Time will pass and the urgency to change will either shrink or disappear into lives where we settle. I don't know about you, but I don't want my college-aged kids to be sitting in their hip coffee shop, chatting with their friends about their mom, and saying, "Yeah, my mom, she was a good mom, but she settled."

Nor do I want to sit with my friends when my home is an empty nest and say, "I just don't know who I am anymore."

You are worth not settling.

But you have to decide not to assume that you always have tomorrow to do what you need to do today. I know you didn't intend to forget yourself. I know you want to be happy. I know you want to fight for your heart. I know you want to rightly order your life. I know you want to have that deep bravery and sense of purpose. I know you want to rediscover your passions from your childhood.

It's not that we're trying to forget ourselves. We just get busy.

And it's so easy to lose track of time in motherhood. It's even easier to overlook the importance of our own hearts.

I know I did.

Stop saying, "I'll get to that tomorrow." That's our first task for ourselves.

You owe it to yourself, your family, your friends to live without fear and with wild abandon. You owe it to yourself to get to everything on your tomorrow list today.

I am passionate about helping you ignite the fire of urgency in your life. I believe in you, I really do, and know that whether you have one child or fifteen, are married or divorced, are wealthy or poor, have direction or none, you can recapture time's inches in life.

You are worth fighting for each inch today.

2

Pay No Attention to the Mom Behind the Curtain

I grew up in church. I was the good church girl, the good daughter, the one who rarely got in trouble, the one with good grades, the one always smiling.

Church was also where I learned to hide.

For many years I lived the life of the Pharisee who proclaimed her own goodness, while deep down I felt broken and battered. I knew I was pretending, yet there I was, telling everyone how my life was fine and giving advice to others, all while feeling trapped in my good-girl journey.

I started this journey when I was about five. My parents were church planters. They not only started the church I grew up in but also were instrumental in founding the Christian high school I attended. For many years, this starter church didn't have its own building, so we met every Sunday in an American Legion hall. We'd arrive early and enter a dark lower-level room that was in complete disorder with beer cans and cups scattered about, floors sticky with spills, and sometimes vomit outside the door. My job was to help set up metal folding chairs in neat rows before the churchgoers arrived.

I was to take chaos and create order. In some ways I hid the reality of the place behind neatly lined-up rows and emptied beer cups. Church, even then, was a form of pretending.

I remember the smell of stale beer and cigarette smoke that, no matter how well I ordered those chairs, would linger in the background. Outside of everything I did to hide the bones of the building, the smell would always speak truth. But despite the facility, every Sunday morning people would spill through the doors, grab their photocopied bulletin, find a seat, and worship in the transformed room. I tried to stay focused on the metal cross we'd put on the makeshift altar at the front of the room or the changing colors of the altar fabrics, yet sometimes as I shifted around in that metal chair, tucked in the middle row, I'd spy a plastic beer cup still holding the remnants of beer that one of the morning setup staff missed. More often than not, it would be on the shelf behind the altar, precariously perched and waiting to be knocked over, breaking the illusion of holy with worldly.

On one side of the building, off the main room with the metal chairs, were creaky wooden stairs leading to another entryway. Everyone made a grand entrance or exit on those stairs due to their central location and creaky sound. Those stairs taught me to be the good girl—the one who never got in trouble, who never broke rules—because one Sunday when I grew weary of counting hidden beer cups or sitting and standing for the psalms, I started to fidget in that folding chair. I must have created enough of a ruckus, because I suddenly became the girl being taken out of the meeting area by my dad and up the loud stairs while everyone watched.

I was so embarrassed. I don't think I even cared that much about what my dad said to me in that upper hallway. I hated the moment we walked back down those stairs and I stepped into that room, with everyone looking and with my little ego totally busted.

In that moment, I began the good-girl act.

I didn't start behaving in church because I *wanted* to be the good girl; I started behaving in church because I didn't want anyone else to hear those stairs and to think of me as anything *other* than the good girl.

I became the good girl because I cared so much about what others thought of me. Maybe you are a good girl too, or maybe you wear some other mask that you hide behind. It's another tension we live with—we believe it keeps us safe, but it also keeps us from living to our fullest capabilities.

I spent most of my life trying to fix the outside, the story that everyone saw. But spending so much energy on that kept me from fearlessly investing in who I was really meant to be. When I got married and had children, I had another "allowed" excuse for turning off my own dreams and talents, and I dove in fully to being a wife and mom. I need you to understand that devoting yourself to your family is a beautiful, wonderful, and expected part of your journey. This isn't about abandoning your life; this is about reclaiming it and being brave enough to live the real you.

My marriage was a deep struggle. Finances were a continual issue, resulting in anger, passivity, and rejection. At first it was just the normal struggle of a couple starting out. But as the years went on and we sank deeper and deeper below the poverty line, our money struggles moved from normal to critical.

However, I continued to make excuses and carry on as though all was fine, even as we endured a decade of debt collectors showing up at our door, having our truck repossessed, and bankruptcy.

To the world, I appeared put together and happy, never letting anyone see the late notices, dozens of jobs taken and lost, and despair. These were the painful places of me screaming into a pillow in my room, hoping for a break, while my toddlers cried downstairs and the laundry waited to be folded.

Often the tears were of shame and fear. I desperately wanted to let others in, to hear that I wasn't alone, but I was afraid of what everyone would think. Have you ever felt that way? Have you ever experienced shame with regard to your story?

Clinging to the masks, being afraid to admit what is broken, is isolating.

I understand the lonely place.

I also understand that the one thing you need to hear when you're in that lonely place is that *you will be okay*. But okay might not be easy even though it is right.

Some unmasked truth: My marriage of seventeen years ended. When I divorced, I also unearthed $65,000 of debt. I moved from being a home-schooling, stay-at-home mom to being a traveling, working, entrepreneur single mom.

The good-girl act? This certainly wasn't what I had signed up for.

No longer was my life incongruent—like beer cups in church—but rather for the first time, there I was, exposed and vulnerable in my own story.

THOSE MASKS SEEM TO SERVE A PURPOSE

Prior to living in Tennessee, where I now live, I was a Minnesota girl. What am I saying?—I'll always be a Minnesota girl. Our Minnesota house had cute white shutters and a nice porch out front. It also had this fantastic oversized garage attached to it. When my family first moved there, we emptied the contents of our old home into the garage and slowly moved everything we needed into the house. As with any move, when you fill a new space, you end up with things that no longer work, and since the garage was giant, I left the remnants in there.

Over the years, however, that twenty-by-thirty-foot garage became my burden. What once represented freedom and space was crammed so tightly with stuff that I joked how I could have volunteered my garage for an episode of *Hoarders*. That's the show in which professionals show up at a person's home and the person meets them at the door, looks normal, smiles, and then opens the door to an overflowing nightmare of stuff. Mine was never *Hoarders* gross, but it was bursting. Joking about it made me feel better, as though I weren't quite so out of control with the boxes. Oh, I could rationalize back then that it wasn't *that* bad, that there was order to the piles, but I would have been excusing the reality. It may have been organized, but it was still mountains of things.

For example, beyond the regular stuff from moving that we never cleared out, I saved almost all my oldest daughter's artwork from ages three to five. (At one point I realized saving it all was ridiculous but still didn't get rid of those boxes of preschool art.) This included crayon draw-ings on the back of church bulletins and scratches on napkins from res-taurants. That artwork made it into a box on the top shelf of the garage next to a box of my college stuff, a box of wedding stuff, a box of artwork from my next daughter (Chloé), boxes with unpaid bills and statements, boxes of outgrown clothes, toys the kids no longer played with, and more stuff I boxed up, didn't label, and no longer knew why I saved, yet there it was, taking up space.

I despised that garage. When I'd pull into my driveway, I knew what was behind that perfect white door. I was embarrassed by what was inside and worked to hide it from my neighbors. At times, I envied the open garage doors in my neighborhood and determined my neighbors must have it all together since they could freely open theirs without worry. It's not that I didn't have a clue how to fix it or how to let go of what was inside; I just was unsure of how to start and instead put the garage on the list of things to take care of "tomorrow," when I hopefully would have more time and resources. I wanted it finished immediately and got overwhelmed by the seemingly infinite number of steps (which included opening that garage door) to cleaning it out.

There was *just so much stuff to deal with.*

Over the course of many years, I spent days sorting it, moving it, restacking it, organizing it, and attempting to control it. I knew exactly what I was going to donate and what I wanted to junk. Let me tell you, garbage hauling and junk removal isn't always free or convenient. And because I didn't have the money to pay for someone to come haul it away and because there wasn't a free dump site, the stuff accumulated.

There came a day when I no longer allowed my kids to open the garage.

That should have been a sign that help was needed. I ignored the issue, believed it to be an acceptable reality, and made a new family rule: if the kids wanted their bikes, we would open the garage door about three feet, duck under, grab the bikes, and duck back out. This involved one of my kids standing at the garage door opener and opening and closing it for me while I shouted, "Okay! Push the button now!" But before we'd even begin our garage-door ritual, I would walk outside and assess who was around, and if the coast was clear, we'd begin the bike-removal process.

I probably have scars from all the times I misjudged how low I needed to duck and ended up scraping the top of my back in my rush to avoid having neighbors see that space. If this wasn't hiding, then I don't know what is.

Hiding Isn't Painless

If you're hiding, I know you understand. If you're in a financial mess and a birthday party invite comes and you have to figure out a present—and your kid is complaining about the "smallness" of the present that you can't afford but scraped together enough change to buy—it's easy to snap. I've done it. I've screamed in the closet with a pillow over my face. Hiding frays nerves, removes the sheath and the buffer, and eventually traps us into doing irrational things like making rules that the garage door can no longer be opened.

Now, if you had met me back in those married hiding years, you might have thought differently about me. You might have seen the house with the porch out front (which often held the bikes to avoid garage drama), the mom who homeschooled her kids (but was deeply exhausted), the mom with the Suburban (parked conveniently in front of the garage), the mom running from activity to activity never seeming frazzled (who drank so much coffee just to keep going). You might have seen me volunteering (because I felt I had to), serving cookies at church (my turn on the list), driving to ballet (where I volunteered)— always seeming as if I had the strength of an army (remember, the coffee).

You would have seen what I wanted you to see.

It was a grand act, a grand illusion, a space where I worked desperately to keep people from seeing the real me. In some ways, I was like the wizard in *The Wizard of Oz* when he yelled at everyone to "pay no attention to that man behind the curtain."[2] Well, my curtain wasn't just the garage; it was all the masks I decided to hold up so I might fit in.

Let me pull down the curtain so you can really see me. That home with the white shutters and front porch? That wasn't our own but rather a home my parents bought for my family when we were out of options. Despite promising my parents the mortgage would come out of our checkbook, we never made one payment in ten years. Think about that. Ten years. Ten years of my dad opening his checkbook and writing a check to a mortgage company. But on the outside? You never would have seen that our beautiful house was not our own. You also wouldn't have known that ballet, where my daughters excelled, was also given to us because we lacked money and that all my above-hinted-at volunteering, despite exhaustion and lack of time, was my trying to repay the debt and soothe my guilt. You wouldn't have known that I was burned out from homeschooling but afraid of sending my kids to public school and that just thinking about it made me feel that I had failed. You wouldn't have known that I begged and pleaded to get help for IRS audits but was pushed away. Just so you know, don't ever run from the IRS. Call them. Hiding from them *never* works.

There are so many variables to protect when you hide your life from others. Making sure your guard is always up is a scramble. Now, ponder this: Are we not taught that "the hide" is acceptable when we are young? We're expected to put our best selves forward. We are told, "Put on your Sunday best," "Get a new shirt for pictures," "Make sure you hug Aunt Ruth" (when you knew she smelled of that superpowerful rose perfume that made you gag). As a result, we grow up and enter adulthood, keeping up the "required" masks.

Now, as I continue the bare-all of my life, you also need to know that in those years, I would rarely allow anyone to come in through our front door. I'm not joking. If you came over, you'd be lucky to make it to the porch with the bikes. I was afraid that if you entered, you might have seen the real, not-always-put-together me. I didn't want you to see the tattered and ripped plaid couch with the throw blanket perfectly placed over the seam that had exploded, the house with the piles of shoes by the door because our front closet was woefully small, and the bills stamped Final Notice on the counter. I rarely let my kids have friends over, and if their friends brought them home after visiting at *their* house, I'd conveniently meet them on the front porch before they could get to the door.

If you decide to implement this hide, which I don't want you to do, you must understand that meeting someone on the front porch means that for the fifteen minutes before they arrive, you are standing in the living room, waiting, watching for them to show up. In those moments, my time wasn't spent doing anything other than protecting the hide.

What could I have done with my time spent on the mask holding? Have you ever thought about that part? Every moment you give to keeping up appearances and keeping a mask on is a moment you are taking from another area of your life. Even if it wasn't for personal growth, what if it was time with your kids? Or cleaning the kitchen? Or just resting? Hiding harms only one person: you.

One of the scariest moments can be when you start to look at all the places you hide. It can be humbling to admit that you're unhappy or that there are problems or that you have been pretty passive in your life. But you can't fix anything until you admit that you hide.

In order for me to clean out the garage, I couldn't do a thing until I *opened* the door. And just so you know, not one neighbor laughed at me when I did. No one put signs on my yard labeled Hoarder Lives Here. Do you know what happened? My next-door neighbor John saw me hauling junk out and started to help me. He brought his truck, and we loaded stuff in it and drove to the dump. He didn't chide the hide—he stepped into my space and helped me break free.

You have to believe me here. Hiding is a gigantic weight on your life. There's not much freedom in walking around dragging weights with you. And it's exhausting trying to keep the illusion maintained. Do you know what is on the other side of hiding? Freedom.

I can't make you put down your masks. *This is up to you.* I can share my story—my ups and just as many downs. I understand how hard change is, and I can tell you how I limited my potential. And that I could not change *one* thing until I decided I wasn't going to live behind the curtain, holding the masks, anymore.

There is so much awesome in just being you.

Letting Go of That Image

If you want to experience joy, if you want to stop pretending and be real, then it will require something from you. You will have to let go of that facade, that mask, or the good-girl (or bad-girl) image you've clung to. It will require that you change.

Change isn't easy.

I had to evaluate *who* I was and every excuse I'd used for being *where* I was in life. Even now, sharing honestly about that time and how I hid is difficult for me. But it's important that you understand the broken-down me. So often we see just the after in a person's life and don't get to know the before, the person inside, the person behind the masks. But I know that if you can see the before me, the me who tried to be good enough, the me who was stuck, you can understand the necessity of change and getting *your* life back to who God created you to be.

I became the woman standing in the middle of her life with nothing but hope, faith, and bravery to reclaim her ticking timeline of days on this earth. This wasn't when I was twenty without kids but rather when I was in the busiest season of motherhood, when there didn't seem to be a moment for self or for change. I no longer had the luxury of living behind excuses but was *forced* to change my life. And in that place of brokenness, I found not only life and hope but also faith again.

Your life and experiences are different from mine. Don't compare your normal or your dramas with mine; instead, see if my stories unearth parallels in your own journey. But know this: I bet there are places where you hide too. I want you to start looking at what you hide behind. What are those things? What keeps you from removing the masks and living in the light of freedom?

I know it's scary to venture into the unknown. I know that first step toward real and positive change can be terrifying. But I also know you can find joy on the other side.

By the way, the best way to never have your garage reach *Hoarders* status and having some cable-TV-show producer reach out to you is to keep your garage open. The same goes for hiding. Once you put the mask on or accept the good-girl label, it's much harder to take it off.

Live openly, proud of the entire you.

And clean out your garage.

3

Sticks and Stones

When my kids were little, I spent hours and hours reading to them. Though reading the same children's books over and over wasn't my favorite thing, I forced myself to read them for the greater good. Honestly, I found many of the books annoying—particularly the picture books without plots that were only popular because some fashion doll or superhero was on the front. I did read a few books I probably loved more than my kids did. *The Story About Ping* and the entire Little House on the Prairie series made their way onto the Mom-Approved List of Reading Awesomeness, so I'd sneak those into the pile for us to read. It was only fair, after all, that we read some books that didn't make me inwardly groan, as I did when I read about Barbie giving life lessons on friendship.

One book everyone clamored for—especially my oldest son and number four child, Brennan—was *You Are Special*, by Max Lucado.[3] Lucado has this parable quality of writing to express truth or a life principle through a story that speaks to our hearts without the use of gimmicky characters. In this story, Lucado wrote about Punchinello, who was a Wemmick. The Wemmicks carried around a collection of dots and stars they used to grade one another, and not in a good way. If any Wemmick saw a "friend" doing something deemed not cool, he had the authority to place a dot on that individual. But on the flip side, if the Wemmick liked the other individual, he could give him or her a star. In their culture, they wanted the "good life" and needed to avoid the dots and collect the stars.

Punchinello was a dot-covered mess of a Wemmick. Some people even placed dots on him just because he had dots. No matter how hard Punchinello tried to ignore those dots, they started to weigh him down. You can see it in the illustrations: the slumped shoulders, the sadness on his face, the shuffling steps. Punchinello believed he was worthless, a failure, but more than that, he didn't know how to identify himself beyond his society-driven, dot-covered identity. He longed for the stars, but based on the extraordinary number of dots he wore, he believed he would never receive one.

One day Punchinello met another Wemmick without a dot *or* a star. She was happy and joyful, and he wondered about her no-dot-sticking secret. She told him about the creator and said that Punchinello needed to meet him too. The creator—a kind old carpenter, mirroring God—gently explained to Punchinello how he created each Wemmick with unique beauty, skills, and talents. Punchinello questioned all the dots he was wearing and tried to justify his worthlessness because of the exceptional number of dots and lack of stars he had.

The creator chuckled, like we do as loving parents, then looked Punchinello in the eyes and told him that he didn't make mistakes and that others cannot define his value. Punchinello was loved for who he was deep down in his heart, not for what his society decided he was worth. As Punchinello left the creator's home—and this is the part that chokes me up—the dots began to fall off his once weary, socially-defined-as-a-mess-up body. Instead of holding his head low, concerned about what others thought of him, he bravely lifted it high, his face filled with joy. The moment he didn't let someone else define him was the exact moment his dots fell off. No longer was a dot able to stick to his body because *now* Punchinello understood that his worth wasn't defined by others' ridiculous grading system but rather by his heart, which was deeply loved by his creator.

We're a world of Wemmicks. Whether we verbalize it or not, all those social apps on our home screen are like that public grading system. A like, a heart, an angry face. I suppose we could attempt to isolate ourselves from the digital space, but the reality is it's harder and harder to create that margin from the online world. The deep struggle happens when we're in the midst of lives that are challenging while the world keeps adding dots and forgetting to give out stars.

I freely admit that I've struggled over those virtual dots. I've deleted posts on Facebook when they didn't get the engagement I wanted. And sometimes I get frustrated and jealous about the number of likes someone else gets. It's easy to use it as a grade of worth. Think about how effortless it is to question validity of self, appearance, and success regarding online posts. Have you ever put up a picture of yourself, thinking how great you look in it, only to have hardly anyone reply? And then when there are only a handful of likes, you decide there must be something wrong with the picture and thus take it down? Social media is our Wemmick-like approval world. It's easy to let either the "silence" or the "noise" online act as marks of beauty, success, value, importance, and validity.

In fact, masks are approved.

Communicating our stories with the world now consists of carefully edited, filtered, and curated images and words. Think about the number of filters on Instagram and Snapchat. While designed for fun, they also distort the real person behind the image. We're subtly told, *Don't be the real you. Add stuff, make silly faces, smooth your skin.*

Is there any doubt so many of us feel like Punchinello? Heavy, weighed down, covered in dots, longing for a star?

If you're sitting there feeling as if you can't keep up with society's expectations and also struggling with the role of motherhood coupled with your own loss of self, you need to understand you're not alone. It's so simple to fall into believing that value can be defined by others, but it's critical to remind yourself that the external grading system is not allowed to stick on your identity. For us to get to a place of change, however, we have to come to a moment when we stop and say, "Enough." Then, instead of just accepting labels, we need to be ruthless and honest with ourselves and rip those dots off.

When we accept the dots as fact versus ridiculousness, we aren't valuing our own hearts. All those labels—whether we've fallen flat on our faces and our lives are a mess or not—don't define who we really are. In fact, all they do is keep us stifled.

THE GREAT COSMETICS-AISLE INCIDENT

When I was in sixth grade, I carried on myself a collection of self-worth dots and stars. I already strived for the "good girl" star and desperately avoided the dots. I was a preteen, quite awkward and insecure. Some days I'd go to school ready to find out what the next dot would be, and instead of fighting it, I accepted it without question. To make things worse, I also went through the unavoidable worst-haircut-in-the-world phase. My hair was a cross between Carol Brady of *The Brady Bunch* and a frizzy eighties mullet. Think short hair on the side, long hair in the back. It was bad. Even now I still put dots on that picture.

Hair aside, I did try to be outwardly put together and persuaded my mother to spend a ridiculous amount of money on name-brand items so I could fit in. Truthfully, I was trying to overcompensate for the haircut and hoped being on trend would earn a star for effort.

This trend included a pair of floral splotchy leggings. Those pants, for my twelve-year-old self, were glorious. Imagine high-waisted, skintight neon workout leggings crossed with bold geometric patterns made to appear like flowers, and you have an image of the awesomeness of my pants. Somehow, despite my awkward appearance, those leggings had the ability to make me feel as if I were the coolest kid on the block, ready to meet the cutest boy in the mall. I always paired them with my favorite white oversized sweatshirt and my Keds shoes. I'd polish those blue Keds tabs on the back to make sure everyone could see I wasn't wearing knockoffs but the real, star-approved deal.

One confidence-soaring Wednesday, when I was wearing the "killer" outfit, my mom took my family to Target. I begged to walk around by myself because back then I had no interest in laundry detergent, garbage bags, and electronics. After my mom relented, I broke away from the household section, made my way past linens, and bravely entered the gloriousness of the cosmetics aisles. In those moments, I felt like the queen of that Target. Now my biggest decision, as I stood facing the tubes of Maybelline lip gloss, was deciding which color I wanted: bubblegum pink or fuchsia flood red.

"Hey, ugly."

I looked up. Looked to the left, saw no one.

"Hey, ugly."

Okay, this was weird, especially for the cosmetics aisle, where all the stuff is there to make you not feel ugly. So I looked up again. To the right, at the end of the row, was a group of junior high boys, and they were laughing.

I turned around to see who the intended target was.

No one stood behind me.

Oh, the horror. Now the fuchsia red flooded my face.

My ego was crushed, all the stars I wore fell to the floor, and the girl who moments prior was vying to be queen of the local Target now wore a gigantic "ugly" dot. I didn't care about lip gloss anymore. I just wanted out, wanted to get in the car, wanted to escape.

As we drove home that day, I didn't tell my mom what had happened. I didn't want to listen to her telling me about how rude those boys were. I was too embarrassed, too ashamed of the dot.

I never wore those pants again. But my heart? It wore that "ugly" dot those boys gave me. Decades later those boys surely had forgotten about the great cosmetics-aisle incident, but my heart sure hadn't.

After that day, I made a couple of subconscious decisions about myself: (1) it's not safe to share with those who love me things that are embarrassing, and (2) society decides my worth. These are heart agreements. A heart agreement is like a contract that dictates our responses. Even though none of those things were true, especially that pimply faced teen boys can define beauty, the heart, left unchecked, can easily override the brain's logic and accept irrational, unwise, and incorrect agreements about self, beauty, worth, and ability. When those boys called me ugly, I freely accepted their words as a defining dot and began to live with that agreement as my reality. I believed I was ugly.

I carried that "Hey, ugly" dot for most of my life. It made me look twice at the clothes I wore, made me think I needed filters to be seen, and made me quick to accept society's labels.

We make agreements with ourselves from childhood and throughout our lives regarding our responses, our futures, and our capabilities. Just like a legal contract, our agreements are areas we bind ourselves into living out. Eventually these agreements creep into our identities and have the potential to either keep us on positive trajectories (*I am beautiful*) or hold us back (*I am ugly*). They become the stars and dots that dictate our self-worth.

Many agreements we choose to believe are positive:

- I will not let fear dictate my response to this situation.
- I am worth speaking my heart.
- I am a good mom because I try hard.

But others are damaging:

- A good mom doesn't work outside the home.
- A good Christian woman doesn't get divorced.
- I will keep all my stuff because I might not be able to replace it.
- I am a better person if I do everything on my own.
- I am ugly.

Even now, at over forty years old, it's hard for me to accept hearing someone tell me I look beautiful. I'll immediately search for a flaw, for a reason to discount that person's words. As I've gotten older, I've had to wrestle with how beauty isn't outer but rather is a combination of our outside and inside worlds. That means I must look squarely at the agreement I made with myself when I was twelve and decide to no longer be bound by the dots of others but to be bound by real truth.

The dots people put on us don't have to remain there. But too often, just as I did with my twelve-year-old self, we keep those dots there and believe that we deserve them; that we're ugly, stupid, unfit, unworthy, untalented; that we are failures; that we cannot change.

Can you imagine telling your fifth grader who is struggling in math that she is a big failure? She comes home and shows you the paper with the red mark on it, and out of your mouth comes, "Well, you're a failure. You'll never get math. Ever. Here, take this gray dot and wear it always to remind yourself of how much you stink at math and how you'll never figure out those seven multiplication facts. What a loser." We would never do that to our kids. Even when we cannot believe that "six times seven equals forty-two" hasn't become cemented in their brains. We don't add the dots on them because we love them beyond that fact, but more than that, we understand that the words we say stick.

If our kids came home and told us someone said they wouldn't amount to anything, we'd refute it. We'd sit them down and tell them they should never allow someone's words, those sticks and stones, to break them. If one of my kids told me someone had said "Hey, ugly" to him or her, I'd be clear that those words were lies. You'd do the same.

Yet in our own lives, we accept the labels for our perceived failures without a second thought. But even more powerful, more important, and often hidden are the dots we give ourselves:

- My house is a crazy mess. Dot.
- My laundry is never caught up. Dot.
- Sometimes I yell at the kids. Dot.
- The kids are behind in math and it's my fault. Dot.
- I have overdue bills. Dot.
- Sometimes I don't like being a mom. Dot.
- I feel overwhelmed. Dot.

It's a brave thing to look at those dots—the ones other people have given us and the ones we have given ourselves—and acknowledge that they aren't truth. We aren't failures when we make mistakes or miss a payment or want some kid-free time. We aren't mess-ups when we desire to pursue talents that are apart from motherhood or wear flowery (and awesome) leggings. No one can create agreements in our hearts without our approval. Let me repeat that to you: No one can create agreements in *your* heart without *your* approval.

When you begin to love the core you, the one underneath the dots and stars, then, just like for Punchinello, the labels will not be as sticky. It doesn't mean you'll never have a moment when one of those dots sticks. It instead means you are aware that your identity is beyond them. In fact, it is your responsibility to yourself to lead those false self-agreements to truth. You don't have your mom redirecting your thoughts; you have you. Sometimes even now, if I'm struggling with worth, I ask myself, *Would my mom tell me that?* And when the answer is clearly no, I know that dot should be discarded.

Do not allow those dots to remain for one more day.

You are not ugly.

You are worthy.

It's time to start believing it.

4

Will the Real You
Please Stand Up?

Early in my marriage, when our first three kids (Hannah, Chloé, and Grace) were all under the age of five, we lived for one winter in San Diego. Moving from the frozen tundra of Minnesota to a state where the weather extremes involved upper sixties to upper seventies was fantastic and eye opening and fun. San Diego was going to be our fresh start, which we already needed, as our financial woes were deep and suffocating. So when a job for my husband opened in San Diego and we moved there, I fully believed that paradise-like city was the answer to my prayers.

Life was going to be different.

I worked hard to do new things: I explored the ocean, drove across the mountains, met new people. The cool thing was that in the months prior to moving, I decided I was going to enter my new world with a completely blank slate. My mask? It wasn't that I didn't let others know we didn't have money; I just refused to let them know *why* we didn't have money. In fact, at my church in Minnesota, I had established myself as the gal with the prayer requests that never ran out, where the jobs weren't secure, and she needed help. Instead of clinging to the deep fear that our life was going to implode, I dared to believe this time life would be good.

I had a mindset of hope.

During our time in San Diego, on Tuesday mornings the kids and I would trek across the mountain range from our home in Rancho Bernardo to a church overlooking the Pacific Ocean to attend a Bible study. This church was tucked in a neighborhood of million-dollar homes and women with nannies and lives of perceived perfection. The church was beautiful and different from anything I had experienced. When I first started attending the Bible study, I was the girl who moved from Minnesota, the one who said bag with the long *a* sound, the girl waiting to get settled here, the girl with opportunity on the horizon, the girl with three little girls. I thrived on being the one finally not pitied but the one who could sit in the circle during prayer-request time and offer superficial requests worthy of a gal who lived the good life.

On the first day of our study, I was late because I had to drop the kids off in new nursery settings. As a result, I walked into the fellowship hall and saw almost completely full tables. Instead of walking confidently over to the first open seat, I stood in the back, assessing the women at each table. I'll admit it—I was looking for a group of people who looked as though their lives weren't perfect. Don't pretend we don't do that, because at some point most of us assess. Let me remind you, I was in the neighborhood where my four-year-old green Plymouth Voyager stood out like a sore thumb in a parking lot of Bentleys, Mercedes, and BMWs. And it was a minivan, which carries a stigma of its own. If you are a minivan owner, I know you get this.

"Miss, do you need a table?" a kind old man asked me. I looked at him, wondering if he knew I was judging everyone, and nodded as color crept into my cheeks. He then gently gestured toward a table on the right side.

That table was the first one I had eliminated.

No, no, no, no! Not the table with all of them! They all appeared too perfect, too blond, too wealthy, too non-minivan driving for me to ever fit in.

"Sure, that table is great." That's what I told him while I inwardly groaned.

Each Tuesday for six weeks, I walked to that side table, sat with the women who seemed to have put-together lives, and despite my insecurities and lack of financial security, I seemed to fit in. They welcomed me, but we all just stayed as see-you-on-Tuesday church-level friends. I told them the highlights of my story, how moving here was a risk but I had faith and that despite my money being limited (especially compared to theirs), I knew it was just a "season."

In case you are wondering, calling struggles a "season" may seem to be an easy way to dismiss long-term stuck, but a season should last for, well, a season. Three months, not eighteen years. My "season" seemed to be never ending. Along with masking my problems behind the word *season,* I made sure my prayer requests seemed to be from a gal without a care in the world, not stuck in a cycle of poverty. Going to a new church allowed me a moment to feel normal, as if I had it together. But as the weeks passed, my "new" life crumbled more and more behind what I shared.

When you have heart issues that need addressing, you can't just rearrange stuff around you. You have to get to the root of not only *why* but *how* the problem happened and then *work* to fix it. Our move to California never addressed the deeper issues of responsibility, respect, marriage, and control. Collection notices still came, even with the address change. Obviously you cannot escape problems by running from them. Daring to hope that life will change and daring to do the things to change it are completely different. So without the mental modifications of change, I found myself back in the same spot as before: after several months and after signing a year lease on a $1,750-a-month town house, my husband lost the job I had believed was God's answer to prayer.

The night after I found out he had lost his job, I sat on the hill next to our town house and cried. My dreams were thwarted. My hope wasn't even lost—worse, I felt foolish that I had dared to hope when we crossed the state line. I didn't want to walk back into the house; I wanted to get into the van and drive far, far away. It was hard to breathe, hard to see beyond the embarrassment of the moment and the ramifications of failing. Life felt too hard, honestly, and I didn't want to have to muster up the strength and humility to survive this again. But just as moms do, I dug deep for my kids and walked up the stairs into our home. I didn't quit but tried again.

Again.

This is one of those points when we come face to face with keeping on—when the weight of change, the weight of life, the weight of reality seems heavier than we can bear. Those last days in San Diego were oppressive because of not only the shattered dreams but also the anger I felt at myself—that I'd allowed myself to hope. Remember how I called hoping foolish? In those moments sitting on the hill, I didn't just beat myself up with the worry of no longer having money to pay the bills; I also beat myself up for being foolish to think things could change.

I felt isolated and alone. I couldn't call home, couldn't bear to share with our friends and family who had cheered us on when we took the risk that fell apart within four months. And none of my friends in San Diego knew about that previous financial roller-coaster part of my life.

How was I going to walk into my new church, the church where I tried to live out of the paradigm of our new existence, and admit to those there that my life was collapsing?

The next morning was Bible study day. I absolutely did not want to be in my town house—it now felt suffocating with the realization we would be losing it—so I packed up my girls, drove across the mountains, and walked into the fellowship room. Even humbled, I still went to a place of strength: with my friends. I think it is very easy to dismiss the strength we have and the power of others, but that day I knew that's where I needed to be and used that strength to carry me.

That Tuesday, on the sixth week of our study of *The Purpose-Driven Life*, I walked over to the table where it felt like the deepest prayer request was for "the strength to get all the packing done before my trip to Paris" and sat my beat-up self down. I slapped on the she's-got-it-all-together smile because I didn't want these friends to know the real me. I tucked my pain as deep as I could because I still believed that if they really knew me, the reality of everything crumbling again would be real. I tried so crazy hard not to let go, tried to hide those tears, tried to be strong. Until prayer time.

Oh, trust me, I started out with a safe surface request, but this day my heart beat out my pride.

THE DAY MY GRIP GAVE OUT

I'm an ugly crier. I know we all say we are ugly criers, but let it be known that I am an ugly, record-quality-of-horror crier. My nose runs as much as the tears, and my face gets mottled and swells up. If there were an award for Worst Puffy Face After Crying, I'd win. To make it worse, I always seem to have crying fits at the most inopportune times, like before teacher conferences or family pictures. And then, because of the award-winning-ugly-crying part of me, I end up being bloated in the face for the next six hours while I sit across from someone, hoping he or she doesn't notice the red-rimmed eyes and blotchy face.

On that Tuesday morning, during prayer-request time, after I probably asked for the funds for a new stroller, I tried superhuman strength to force those tears welling up not to fall, but that was the day of ugly crying in the midst of perfection. The more I willed the tears back, the more my bottom lip quivered, and at a certain point, pride's grip gave out. Instead of finishing my prayer request, my face scrunched up and the full-fledged, award-worthy crying moment began. I can't even say if the women stared at me with gaping mouths, because my eyes were so swollen and everything was blurred. Thank goodness for the fuzzy vision because it keeps us mega-criers in the dark to the immediate response of others. But this day, in the midst of the tears, worn out by life, I took a risk and let pride go. As I cried, I blurted out everything: about not having money, the collectors' notices, the lost job we'd deemed "God's answer to prayer," the countless jobs lost in Minnesota, the bankruptcy several years prior, and my fears of losing everything again. Before I finished, the leader, the most intimidating one with the best hair ever, came over to me. She handed me a tissue, and then as I took it, she hugged me in my messiness. I'm sure those tears stained her several-hundred-dollar shirt, but she didn't care (or at least never backed away).

It was a sacred moment of humanness.

Pretty soon it wasn't just her but the entire table of women who gathered around me, not judging but loving. They held me, wiped my eyes, offered prayers. The mutual love, the fellowship, the letting go—it was enough to stop my flood of tears.

At some point, when I felt as though the focus on me was more than enough, I sat back and looked to my friend on the left and asked her about her request. I sat, swollen faced, trying to slow and hide the deep, loud, spasmodic breaths, awaiting more vacation-and-nanny prayer requests.

And then a cascade ensued.

"I'm going through a horrible divorce. My husband cheated on me."

"No one knows, but he lost so much money. We're showing my house, and my deepest fear is potential buyers will open the fridge and see how I have no food. I'm afraid."

"My son disowned me. He hasn't talked to me in several years, and I found out through a friend he's getting married. I'm so hurt, so angry."

"I am so alone. I don't have any friends I can be real with. I don't know who I can trust, and I'm so tired of pretending."

On and on and on the mask removing went.

Before long our once-chill table was requesting tissues from the next table.

These requests weren't about Europe or nannies or superficial needs. These were real, gut-wrenching prayer pleas from a table of women who, unbeknownst to me, were also holding up their own masks, hiding their stories from everyone. How in the world had we all sat at the table for six weeks and not ever gotten to actually know one another beyond where we like to get coffee? What was so frightening about being real?

As the stories poured out, the sacredness of the space ignited as we unearthed a kindred love for one another. We were all tired of existing alone, we all had areas where we needed help, yet not one of us had dared to admit that we were stuck or afraid.

If everyone pretends to have it together, it's a feat to be the first one who breaks the illusion. But I've seen it happen over and over, the rawness and freedom of real. It happens when one is brave and shares how she needs community, not isolation.

Braveness isn't rooted in perfection or ideal situations. Bravery doesn't get awarded during the smooth-sailing times of life but rather is unearthed in the times when our tears fall, when our strength gives out, when we push beyond what we think we are capable of. Bravery is being strong when there is no other option than being strong. And bravery is admitting we need help.

I honestly didn't think I was being brave that day. I didn't see it until later, until years afterward. In that moment, I was tired and worn out and needed something I didn't have: hope. Now I can see how my story of tragedy and fear, my mask crumbling in tears to the table, was not an invitation to judge but an invitation to love. It was also an invitation to let go of pain and numbness and be real.

In some ways, it might be easy for you to look at your life and decide it's too broken, too normal, too stuck, too without a purpose. But when you have the bravery to set down the perfection and expose your dotted spaces, it is only then that you won't have to spend so much time holding up your masks or sucking in your breath being strong. It takes a risk to be brave, to be real, but that day—when I had cried my hardest in front of all those women whom I had judged as perfect—was the beginning of freedom.

What's keeping you from getting real? Fear? The idea that others might judge you harshly? The sense that if you confess what your life is really like, it will be too difficult to face?

Freedom and bravery don't happen when we hide. They come only when we step into the truth of who we are and what we're facing. If you want to change, if you desire to experience life and rediscover your passions beyond the hiding, dot holding, and constant exhaustion from trying to keep it all together, then it's time to let yourself be real.

One last thing—let me reassure you of this—you are not the only one starting that journey. Over the course of years writing on my blog, it hasn't been only one table of women saying, "Me too." It's been millions.

You can be real. We all believe in you.

5

Survivor

I have been told my whole life that I am strong. Not in the physical sense, despite my willingness to challenge anyone to an impromptu arm-wrestling battle, but in the "It's so great you're so strong, because you can handle so much more than the average person" kind of way. That was exactly the kind of statement I tried desperately not to have attached to me in San Diego.

I didn't want to be strong in dealing with constant struggles. I didn't want to be told it was good I was so strong—truthfully, what other option did I have?

Have you been told you're strong and it's made you cringe?

None of us get through life without some gashes and bruises—those fear-originating places. I need stock in Band-Aid, Gatorade, and Starbucks (for the sanity) to make it through all my drama. We all have places where we've messed up royally. You might have the added trauma of a vanishing retirement or a crumbling marriage. Or perhaps you have stories of infidelity, abuse, or children who are sick or have died. You might not have a good relationship with your folks or siblings.

And do I even need to start with the list of crazy that our kids add to our lives? Many of my Facebook status updates include moments when either my kids did something mind boggling or I was ready to pull my hair out due to the unexpected emergency-room visit or late-again science project.

Simply being a mom makes us strong.

Some of us have kids who once thought we were the best thing since ice cream but now, having hit a certain age, look at us like we're the devil. We have to deal with their rebellion and smart-mouthed comments or their deafening silence. We have to make it through their school years, never-ending homework, questionable grades, and driver's permit.

I mean, come on, we're exhausted, right? There wouldn't be dozens of social media memes about being tired if we all were not collectively spent. Who has time to muster strength to do anything other than making it through? Change, finding ourselves, all of it requires strength, and strength is a commodity we either are tired of having or don't seem to know where to find.

You have this life-changing strength. And now we're going to dig deep and uncover that there isn't just one type of strength but many variations, and you—despite thinking you're too tired, too busy, too lost, too overwhelmed to find any of them—own them all.

CRAZY MOTHER STRENGTH

Last summer I drove my kids from our home in Nashville to Minnesota to spend a week with their dad. During the week they were there, I was in Haiti, working on setting up relationships with missions who work with moms. I know the power of giving back and having others help me out, so during that week, I decided to sit side by side with moms in need, learning how I could provide aid. Beyond the life-altering perspective Haiti brings, it was a good thing for me to be so far away during that time because I probably would have constantly worried about my kids. Isn't that what we do as moms? We worry.

At the end of the week, on a Friday night, I flew back to Minnesota from Port-au-Prince and headed to my parents' house, planning to spend the next day visiting and resting before trekking back to our new home in Tennessee. The kids were going to get dropped off at my folks' house on Saturday afternoon, and then my plan—which everyone called crazy—was to leave early the following morning and drive straight through back to Tennessee. Mind you, this isn't a drive to the mall. This is a fourteen-hour drive with five kids (my oldest two were in college) in one over-packed van with me as the only driver. My parents wanted me to rest at least another day before attempting that drive. I convinced them a good night's sleep was enough for me to make it easily.

Those plans changed quickly the moment my kids arrived at my folks' place. My eleven-year-old, Caleb, walked into the house and started to sob. He rolled up his sleeve, and there on his arm, just above the elbow, was a giant inflamed and very infected cyst. When he touched it, nasty white pus oozed out. Not quite to the level of gross that earns a spot on YouTube, but it was bad. To make it worse, the area was burning hot, and I knew, the way we moms always know, he needed medical care.

This was not how I planned my return home. Part of me wanted to look away and put off dealing with it until the next day. But the tears, the infection, the reality made me dig deep.

Even in the face of exhaustion and trial and scary stuff, we moms rise up and deal.

But I'm also human. I was teary and angry and wanted to scream, "How in the world does one's arm get this bad?" Instead of sitting in indecisiveness and anger, I quickly moved to considering solutions. We were 929 miles from our Tennessee home, from his doctor and our clinic, where our insurance was freely accepted. I knew Caleb's arm needed medical attention as soon as possible, and since school activities were starting Monday, I also knew we *had* to get back.

I couldn't risk mulling over a decision. And in that breath, I decided at 9:48 p.m. that we were going home.

Immediately. Not when I had rest, not when the sun came back out, but *now*.

"Get your stuff! Go to the bathroom. We are getting in the van now and driving home."

Caleb started crying again, but this time because he was so thankful. I can still hear him, sobbing and thanking me for taking him home. None of his siblings argued, no one complained, and there I was, at 10:00 p.m., hauling our belongings to our van, throwing them in the van topper, and preparing to drive from Minneapolis to Nashville. I'd be driving in the dark, overnight, less than twenty-four hours after arriving stateside from serving an extremely tiring week in Haiti.

Before I left, I slathered Caleb's arm with antibiotic ointment, gave him some meds, marked the edge of the welt with a pen, and took photos so I could monitor the borders of the infection and be fully prepared to pull into an emergency room if needed. My mother-bear instinct was in overdrive.

Nothing was going to stop me. Nothing.

Just before midnight, as my van crossed into Iowa, I thought I was crazy. *How in the world am I going to stay awake all night long?*

I had already drunk a double espresso and was working on some Coke to keep me awake, but my eyes were heavy and my body tired.

"Just drive. Just drive. Just drive. Just drive."

I chanted those words over and over and over as the miles ticked by: 145, 158, 203, 300, 358 . . .

It was purely will—mind-over-reality, ferocious determination.

It was the *Braveheart* strength of motherhood.

Sometimes I feel like William Wallace in *Braveheart,* the movie in which Mel Gibson plays one ordinary man who musters the courage to fight and overthrow a nation. That was me, in that van, in the middle of Missouri.

In moments of fatigue, which were many, I'd look back at that almost-twelve-year-old boy, and my heart would be revived with determination. Oh, that momma's fight of ours wells deep at times, doesn't it? When I fell prey to the tired, I'd turn back and look at him, and sheer willpower would return.

Keep driving. Keep awake for Caleb.

The miles kept adding up, the sun rose, and I still pressed on.

I finally pulled into my driveway at 12:32 p.m. on Sunday. Home. But no rest yet.

Despite the tremendous desire to walk up the stairs to my room and fall on the bed, I packed Caleb back into the van. Within forty-five minutes of our family arriving home, the urgent-care doctor took one look at his infected arm and sent us right to the emergency room, where she called to prep for our arrival. Once there we didn't even have to sit down. A bypassing triage nurse heard me desperately explaining the situation to the admissions person, and with one look at Caleb's arm, they took us back to a room with a doctor waiting. Fifteen minutes later, the doctor attempted to numb Caleb's arm and began lancing the cyst.

Watching the agony Caleb had to endure was the worst. Despite the promise that the numbing shots would relieve the pain, they lessened it only slightly. A part of me wanted the hospital staff to just stop, yet I knew Caleb had to deal with the hurt in order to heal.

It took two nurses holding him down and me forcefully and lovingly telling him to breathe to keep him still. It reminded me of when he was born and how my midwife got right in my face. I was exhausted and wanted to quit, but she commandingly said, "You can't quit. You won't quit. You will get through. Stop fighting the inevitable and let your body deliver him."

Now I stared into his eyes—eyes I loved from the moment I first saw him—and told him similar words. "I believe in you. You need to be strong right now. You will get through this. I will not leave you, Caleb."

Those getting-through moments are the times when our real strength is put on the line. They're the moments when we couldn't care less about others watching or what they think. They're the places of love at its rawest and our strength at its most determined. We don't back down when something involves our kids.

Yet sometimes we do when it's about ourselves.

SURVIVAL STRENGTH

You and I have survival strength. Survival strength *deals* with the situation but *does not change* it. Caleb had to use survival strength to make it through his time in the emergency room. I had to use that same strength to drive through the night and walk into the emergency room the next day despite sheer exhaustion. We use that strength when we labor and deliver our children. There is no other option than surviving the moment.

Don't get me wrong; there are absolutely situations in which we must be strong in surviving, but they should be short, punctuated times. Survival strength should not be tolerated long term. In the last years of my marriage, I felt as though I was constantly in surviving mode. *If I can just make it through today,* I'd pray. It wasn't about just making it through the motions; it was about making it through the motions while there were so many problems that needed to be fixed, not ignored, not tolerated. Surviving spaces without trajectory or motivation to change are places where we have *inverted* the power of strength. Rather than using strength to create change, inversion creates stagnation—or in many cases, existing.

For many years, I was really strong at just existing.

Have you ever existed, just hoping to get through? Maybe you wanted to change your circumstances but didn't know how or didn't think you had the strength, so instead you used your strength to survive?

At one time, I wouldn't have equated strength with existing, but I would have been lying to myself. It's like the dead man's float they teach in swimming classes, where you learn how to survive in deep water without a life jacket. The goal of this float is to expend very little physical energy. You convince your body not to swim, which would wear you out, and instead float on top of the water, rotating from stomach to back. Despite it not being a physical-strength activity, the mental strength required is exceptionally high. This skill was designed so you can exist in the water long enough to get rescued. It is about getting rescued, not swimming.

It's passive in regard to movement, but it's active strength we spend on surviving.

For too long I lived out of this kind of dead man's survival strength. I convinced myself it was better not to swim, not to tap into the deep strength of movement, but just to be strong enough in the waiting. Instead of using survival strength for just a bit, to gain perspective and energy, I lived with the mindset of *Just make it through.*

I tolerated life.

STRENGTH OF CHANGE

We have another kind of strength. This is the strength of a mindset that has shifted. It's not only active but also resilient, despite the consequences around us. It's a strength of persistence, of goal setting, of vision, of movement.

When I needed to get Caleb home, I used the raw survival strength coupled with this visionary strength. I visualized us making it to Tennessee, pulling into the hospital parking lot, getting Caleb help, Caleb's arm being healed. Even during the moments when I was tired and thought I was out of my mind, I never questioned my resolve or my determination.

This is the strength of change.

This is the mom who will drive through the night, the mom who will call the bully's parents and tell them their kid needs to knock it off, regardless of the potential backlash. It is the mom who will get out of an emotionally abusive or dangerous marriage. The one who will decide to lose that weight, start a business, become president of the PTA. She exhibits the strength of a fighter, the sheer grit of someone not giving up, not taking no as an option. She is not surviving a situation; she is changing the situation.

Even if you doubt it, you have this strength within you. I am sure that when you look back at your life, you can remember moments that make you think, *How in the world did I survive?*

But how do you use this strength when you're exhausted from just being a mom? How do you tap into it when it's not a crisis moment but is, in fact, a crisis decision? During my run-in with the IRS, I learned that dead-man's-float strength is not accepted as a solution. The only way to fix the money issue, to pay off the debt, was to do difficult things, humble myself, work hard, save money, get a better job, and have an unwavering vision that the arrears would be paid.

That is facilitating change, not waiting to change.

When my kids struggle with homework, I tell them to look at it like the games they play on their tablet over and over again until they solve the puzzle. They are persistent. Obviously they have the patience, the ingenuity, and the creativity to solve a problem they don't yet understand, because for them, there is the reward at the end of winning the game. If they could simply access that thought process for homework and use the capabilities that are already there, the entire homework drama could be different. But they can't use that strength until they change the reason for using it. With the tablet game, there is a reward. With homework, there is the "punishment" of work. The reward is rarely there—it's a chore, drudgery.

The power comes when you can figure out the mindset of the tablet-winning thinking and apply it to the boring, tough, scary situations in which you normally don't use that strength. The ability to survive and be tenacious never leaves; instead, it's your willingness to make that mindset change to be visionary strong.

For my ten-year-old, Elijah, he needed to realize that when he gets frustrated with his game on the tablet, he shouldn't allow the frustration to limit his thinking and options. I have asked him many times, "If homework was the game, how would you attack the issue?" When you are unsure if you have the strength to move forward, the best way to find it is to remember a time when you had strength and figure out not *why* you used the strength but *how* you used it. Maybe your how was in creating the outcome, the reward, of where your strength would lead you. Without that, the strength isn't as strong.

When you first picked up this book and thought, *You know, maybe I do want happiness again,* that was like lacing up the combat boots, getting ready for change. Real strength isn't in passivity; it's in the moment you allow the voice of hope to create a new vision for your tomorrow. You already have the capability to do hard things. And you know you have the survival strength. But you also have the visionary strength that can keep you driving forward, despite the fatigue, the worries, the doubts.

These are the options, the doors you could walk through, the decisions you choose every day. But you need to decide: Survive? Exist? Tolerate? Or be tenacious, ferocious, and brave, fighting for meaning in this life you're blessed to live?

Dare to unearth the potential in pressing toward change and wholeness.

Do you know what makes *Braveheart* powerful? It's the combination of survival strength and visionary strength. You need both—sometimes at the same time. When William Wallace went into battle, he had to have the vision of victory coupled with the ingenuity to survive the battle.

That's the strength of a warrior.

That's the brave art of motherhood.

6

The Future of
Your Present Reality

I call myself the "1 percenter" in regard to life situations. Inevitably, I fit into the statistics of rare things happening to me. In the past year, I dealt with Caleb's emergency-room visit. One of my sons was hit by an SUV while crossing an intersection. He was bruised and learned that sometimes people don't yield in crosswalks, and my momma's heart was bruised for days. And our main drain backed up and flooded the lower level. We had to have an excavator dig out the front yard.

Oh yeah, and my van caught on fire and was destroyed. Yes, my minivan actually caught on fire, which unbeknownst to me started with some smoke under the hood that progressed into flames that engulfed the entire thing within ten minutes of our getting out—as in a massive fireball rushing through the cab. My kids and I all escaped, but thanks to Facebook Live, several of the onlookers videoed the whole thing. When I saw a woman holding up her phone as the fireball that used to be our van burned, I yelled, "Hello, Facebook world!" or something ridiculous to acknowledge how my private tragedy had become extremely public.

And just ten days ago, in the deadline moments of writing this book, I broke my ankle. Ironically, I really can't tell you for sure when or how it happened. The issue didn't just suddenly appear but rather built up gradually over a couple of weeks. It might have happened the day I was walking on a leaf-covered hill and stepped into a hidden hole. That really hurt, but not enough to stop me. I knew something was deeply wrong when, weeks later, it would lock up and I was unable to turn it without excruciating pain. Listen, I experienced labor without meds, so when I use the word *excruciating,* I mean it was unbearable. Several X-rays and a surgeon visit later, I found myself with that left ankle strapped into a brace while the lower half of my body disappeared into the MRI machine.

As I rested there, staring at the word *Philips* on the top of the machine and lamenting my pop-music choice meant to drown out the volume of the MRI, I started pondering the tech's words to me moments before he left me alone in that clinical room. Right before he explained the procedure, he asked if I would be able to hold completely still for more than twenty minutes. I instantly laughed and told him that would be absolutely no problem, because this was a dream: no kids, no one calling my name, no way to do anything but be required to rest and not move.

He chuckled and said, "You won't believe how many moms tell me this is the best rest they've had in years."

Now stop and really think about those words. Getting an MRI means you're injured, taken out of life, and potentially in pain, and we moms who are strapped in that machine are vocally *thankful* for its rest. How many moms did it take before the tech established that moms love MRIs because they can sleep?

Why don't we rest? More than that, why do we need someone else to give us permission to rest? I mean, honestly, that's totally me. I will push and push and push. I rationalized a "broken" normal to be an "acceptable" normal. I didn't want to see the doctor the first time my ankle locked up. I dismissed it, despite lying on the kitchen floor one night and crying in pain as my kids watched. Instead, I told myself to push through.

Then it had to happen several more times before I even called my doctor. Then when I went to the doctor, I kept dismissing it as maybe being in my head, because I was way too busy to deal with one more thing. I ignored all the warnings and didn't want to bother asking anyone for help. In ignoring the warnings, I perpetuated the wrong strength.

Once the images were taken, my ankle showed a lesion on a bone and broken pieces hanging out in my joint. The pain I had dismissed was, in fact, real. My surgeon, upon revealing this, now all of a sudden told me, "We need to schedule you for surgery. How does tomorrow afternoon at four thirty work?"

He didn't care that I had school appointments, book deadlines, and just regular mom stuff on my plate. He saw an immediate problem that unless taken care of right away would cause not only pain but also *more* problems. After the surgery, the surgeon told me the fifteen-millimeter and nine-millimeter fragments that were getting stuck in my joint and locking up movement were the largest he'd seen in five years. He couldn't believe I had walked around and lived with—and dismissed—that pain.

I tend to learn the hard way that ignoring something doesn't fix it but just creates—you guessed it—more problems. Being stubbornly blind to problems or accepting them only exacerbates them.

Look at your own life right now and I'm sure you'll see spaces where you keep dismissing the problems or the pain they cause. Think about the times you tell yourself, "It's not *that* bad," even though inside you're thinking, *I can't deal with this anymore!* You need to be honest with yourself.

Don't join the collective group of moms who think MRIs are a needed treat.

Start to admit where you need help.

Getting help, getting rest—those are good things. You aren't any nobler when you deny yourself.

LISTENING TO THE TRUTH TELLERS

When I was in my thirties, I met Ed, a counselor and a wise, weathered man who'd lived a life of brokenness but found healing when he worked on his mindset. I didn't ever expect to go to counseling, but Ed came and presented a lecture at our church on his method of Christian counseling, and it intrigued me. It was less talk, more action, more results, more "taking captive" thoughts and reclaiming truth. After the lecture was over, a friend of mine paid for me to visit with Ed.

When I first started sharing my story with Ed, most of the time I would dismiss the severity of the issues. I believed they were something I was making up in my head (like I recently did with the ankle troubles), and just like that, I rationalized the problems and struggles as "not that bad." Ed, being trained and ninja skilled in his counseling, knew to look beyond my own rationalizing, and just as the surgeon confronted me, Ed did too. Instead of performing an MRI of my ankle, he performed an MRI of my mindset when he asked me to describe my "normal" and points of discomfort.

Ed could see my life fragments, the places I said were "nothing" or "normal" or "not that bad," and helped me understand that the only way I could get unstuck was to deal with the pieces. Those were the places of financial passivity or where I was afraid to speak up for change.

Let's talk for a moment about being stuck. Stuck can happen when we ignore spaces or fragments that need to be fixed. Most of the time, just to reiterate the beginning of this book, we don't go into the New Year thinking, *You know what I want this year? I want to get stuck. I can't think of anything better than living where all of a sudden I wake up one day and don't know what to do or who I am anymore. Brilliant.* We know that's ridiculous. Yet when we find ourselves stuck, we start to question ourselves and then get really mad at ourselves for getting there.

This is the lesson of the boiled frog, which states that if you put a frog in a pot of cool water and slowly and incrementally turn up the heat, you can boil it without it being aware and jumping out to safety.

Stuck is the same.

Most of the time, we think we're doing what is right. Most of us don't intentionally try to sabotage our own life stories. But then when we turn a blind eye to the spaces where things heat up, we convince ourselves, just as I did with my ankle, that it's not *that* bad.

One counseling day, about six years before my marriage ended, Ed asked me to share my heart, and once again I turned into ugly, swollen-eyes, full-on-crying Rachel. As I shared my saga, the depth of pain of collectors and being overwhelmed, I anticipated another discussion about strength and action steps. I opened up but kept my eyes down and not only talked about my finances but also dared to whisper that word *stuck* to him. I didn't know how to find freedom, didn't know how to manage, especially with young kids needing me every moment and not a dollar in my checkbook and not an attempt of securing a job on the horizon. I was trying to be the good girl, the good wife, and despite all my efforts, my world kept crashing down.

When I finished, I looked up and to my surprise saw Ed sitting across from me just as teary as I was. Seeing him cry made me uncomfortable, because the person I trusted to help me resolve the problems appeared to be equally overwhelmed. Hello, anxiousness. Aren't the counselors supposed to give the advice? Here I was, lost and overwhelmed, and my counselor appeared to be just as lost as I felt.

A good counselor doesn't just give wisdom but also has the ability to understand the perspective of the person in front of him. This is true of Ed, who is a kind empath. He didn't offer cliché words, but rather he got in my heart, which is what facilitated his tears, and attempted to understand how I thought and felt. In it all he heard my struggle and saw my fears.

Ed is compassionate, but he's also a truth teller. He doesn't mince words or hide emotions and has no problem getting in someone's face and calling him or her out. There were so many times he told me to stop ignoring the truth and pushed me to unveil my real fears and share how I actually felt rather than using the filtered, make-it-look-a-bit-prettier words I sugarcoated my life with.

Most of the time, as evident by my stubbornness, I am not particularly fond of others knowing answers for my life. I get feisty and defensive and think, *How in the world do you know how I feel?* But sometimes in moments of despair, of hopelessness, there comes a point when I am desperate for someone to have some type of advice beyond "Thank goodness you are so strong." I need someone in my life to tell me truth.

Truth tellers are invaluable because when we find ourselves in points of crisis, we have tunnel vision regarding answers. The truth tellers become our peripheral vision. They remind us that options, even though they may seem depleted from our perspective, still exist. Ed, with the outside perspective, could see the coping, not the fighting for change I needed to be doing.

Finally, he asked one simple question, which became a life pivot point: "Rachel, when you are seventy, do you think your life will still be like this?"

It was an odd question for me, since I was just in my thirties. Yet without hesitating I told him there was no possible way. I knew I would be free from financial ruin. That was my gut talking, that still, small voice we're all born with. I ignore it often, just like I ignore so much, but it's always there talking, reminding, alerting me.

Ed had taught me to quiet my mind and start listening to the words inside my head, to those gut words. We all have an internal dialogue between our brains and hearts. My internal dialogue screams and shouts at me sometimes, especially when I'm late or the kids are struggling or I have mom guilt about taking care of myself. Have you heard your loud critic voice? Have you paid attention to the voice, accepting it as truth? Or have you challenged your own thoughts?

Listening to your mind and your emotions is an important pivot point of change. You, the core you, are in charge of all your thoughts and emotions. Would you allow your grade-school daughter to drive your car? Absolutely not. But when you allow emotions and thoughts to go unchecked, it's like allowing a child, someone not as trained in the truth, to drive your emotional car.

Our minds are powerful tools that are easy to overlook. Yeah, it might be weird to pay attention to our thoughts, but it's not anything new. In fact, I learned in my childhood years of sitting in that American Legion church that it's necessary to "renew our minds." Renewing our minds means not allowing thoughts to run wild but being in charge of the thoughts and patterns. Part of that requires active listening.

After I told Ed that no, I would not still be stuck when I was in my seventies, he kept with his questions. "Will you be unstuck at sixty? How about fifty?" For each one, I clearly and confidently told him I would be free from those places that held me back.

Then he asked me, "Well, how about when you're forty?"

It was at this moment that I hesitated. You can't hide hesitation from a counselor, especially one as ninja trained as Ed. He understands how to read people's body posture and eyes, and he knew in that moment I was afraid. I didn't need to say anything. My pause and my eyes looking down revealed the truth.

"I don't know, Ed. That's less than seven years from now. I think so, but I don't know how. I want to believe it, but I'm scared." I was terrified of hoping, so much so that I started to debate myself. Ed knew about San Diego and the years after. As a result, he grasped how hard it was for me to hope, to believe, to risk trusting that something could resolve even though we were talking about *seven* years in the future. Not seven days or seven months, but seven years.

To be completely transparent, I was terrified to hope that it could be true, that I could be different and in a different place. My emotions and logic were in a fierce debate.

HOPE BEYOND THE WALLS

Ed could see the debate and forced me to come face to face with my fears. Instead of telling me to change, he asked one simple question: "Rachel, do you know the difference between faith and belief?"

I told him I thought I did, but then Ed explained it to me this way. Faith and belief are two different mindsets. You believe that your house is going to be seventy-one degrees when you set the thermostat to seventy-one degrees. You believe that your bank statement accurately reflects your account balance. You believe that your friend will pick up your child from school every day because she has every single day for two years. You believe that you weigh the amount indicated by the scale and also believe that the doctor's scale will tell you a weight that does not match the lower weight (and correct weight) of your scale at home. You believe that if you knock over the milk, it will spill on the floor and form a puddle. Belief is rooted in what we know; it is a law in life.

Faith is different.

Faith is having hope in a future that does not yet exist.

I didn't have faith in that seven-years-in-the-future existence.

"How did Joseph make it through those thirteen years in the dungeon, Rachel?" Ed asked.

He was referring to the story of Joseph in the Bible, and to be honest, I had never pondered those years in prison. Most of the time when we see successful people, we don't really think about all the moments they struggled, unless we watch a video highlighting their massive change. But every person who has gotten unstuck or undergone a transformation had to start at a place where he or she had to deal with one thing: faith that things would change. Joseph's story is a powerful example of faith.

Some important history for you about Joseph: He was the favored one in his family, which meant he was the chosen one, the one destined to do great things. My kids would call him the spoiled-rotten one, the one who gets the extra ice cream scoop and all the attention, but you get the picture. He was the boy his dad always wanted, the one with the cool mom (because back then, the marriage structure was way different, and his dad had two wives), the boy with the expensive multicolored coat given to him only and none of the other brothers. Needless to say, his brothers weren't fond of him. To make his dicey situation with his brothers worse, during those growing-up years, Joseph had a powerful dream in which all his brothers were bowing down to him. Like any "good" brother, he told his mean brothers how this dream was from God with the purpose of showing him how one day they'd all bow to him. Can you imagine that? The spoiled brother coming down the stairs and telling his already-jealous brothers that now God told him they'd throw themselves at his feet?

Hello, revenge. So as any "good" family would, they threw their brother in a pit and sold him into slavery. Joseph ended up in Egypt working for an influential man named Potiphar. Not wanting to betray Potiphar, he refused Potiphar's wife's advances, and she falsely accused him of rape. Joseph received a life sentence and ended up sitting in jail for thirteen long years. Stop and think about that sentence: life in jail. Joseph did not know the day the door was slammed that it wasn't life but would be thirteen years. And we're not talking some fancy, state-of-the-art prison with all the amenities. This was prison in a foreign country, and the crime he was accused of was against a top government official.

Those years in that pit had to have been bleak, without much hope of getting out. I'm sure he wrestled with anger, frustration, and doubt when he remembered the vividness of the dream from years earlier.

At what point would he have dared to throw away the promise of the dream? At what point did he allow bitterness to creep in? When did he doubt the validity? When did he give up on hope and resign himself to rotting away in the normal that was his new reality? Those years, as challenging as they may have been, were not in vain. I understood how easy it was to feel as though I'd lost years as I, too, in my own life, felt the same emotions as Joseph did.

"Rachel, listen," Ed said. "Joseph had faith in the future he was promised."

Faith is confidence in a future that does not match the present reality.

That last sentence really sank in. Faith is the ability to believe in the dream, the unknown.

I had lost faith in my own life. I clung so tightly to belief in hardship and my ability to survive that I negated the power of faith. Hope is the spark of faith, so when I allowed hope to fade, faith went with it. Remember how in that Bible study in San Diego I became angry that I had hoped? I didn't realize it then, but I had allowed the fear of hope to trump the opportunity of it. That was the debate Ed saw in my eyes when he asked about Joseph. For Joseph to survive those years in prison, he had to have greater faith in a future undefined by the thick dungeon walls surrounding him. That meant he couldn't allow the physical and mental confines of his present to dictate the outcome of his future.

Faith and belief are codependent. Joseph needed faith to move himself forward each day, to trust others, to forge relationships. Otherwise he might have ended everything. But he didn't despair. He had hope. He created friends within the dungeon and became known for his ability to understand dreams, so much so that one day Pharaoh called on him to interpret his own dream. When Joseph was able to give the meaning, not only did it result in his release from prison but he was also given the position as second in command of all of Egypt.

Just to add the final coolness to the story, years later his brothers journeyed from their home in Israel to Egypt to get help and, not knowing that the man in charge was Joseph, bowed in front of him. That was the dream, the future, Joseph was promised years prior.

Ed wanted me to understand that we see Joseph's story from the outside. It's easy to think, *Oh yeah, it worked out for him,* because we *know* it did work out. But do you think this was how Joseph thought his life would play out? That this was the plan?

Joseph didn't know that it would work out when he sat in the dungeon or when he was sold into slavery or accused of rape. Joseph could see only the present moment. And in that, he encountered the same choice you and I have every single day: have faith in the future and grab the opportunity in the moment's inch or accept the current reality as all there is and give up on the dream. Just because he was Joseph and the superhero of Bible stories doesn't mean he didn't have the same internal battle we face.

I got it. There was something about that moment, from Ed's tears to his sincerity of wanting me to see that Joseph wasn't always the Joseph we celebrate but rather was just as human as you and me. He asked me the question about my life again: "Do you have faith that your life will turn around by the time you're forty?"

In that moment, the flicker of faith was ignited, because instead of denying hope, I dared to hope. I needed to refuse to allow the circumstances to define my potential. I desperately needed faith. It didn't mean there wasn't work, wasn't time, wasn't dealing with the fragments. It took Joseph thirteen years to break out of prison. It took me seven years from the time Ed told me those words to know things were different.

I believed him.

I chose faith.

Let me be blunt with you: Do you think your life will change in the next twenty years? Ten years? Five years? Two years? You might be just like I was, hearing all the reasons it will stay the same. That's okay. It's risky to hope, especially if you feel stuck. But I need you to genuinely understand that without hope, without deciding you are worth a life of vibrancy, purpose, and joy, you are choosing to settle.

Can you hope? Just for a moment, for a second?

It does not matter where you start.

What matters more is that you start.

Let me be your truth teller, the person sitting with you who sees all you can do. Instead of thinking about why pursuing your talents won't work or why you can't break free from the stuck places, give yourself just a moment to dare to hope.

You can do this.

I have faith in you.

That's what Ed told me that spring day, and that's what I am telling you now.

7

One, Two, Three . . . Jump!

Elijah is my ten-year-old son. He's number six of seven, and I think God gave him an extra dose of dynamic energy. Actually, I'm wondering if the tenacity-and-fearlessness gene took over for him, just as the extra-sensitive gene did for me. He is a risk taker, loves watching *American Ninja Warrior* and practicing parkour, and rarely does anything by the rules. When he was little, he loved to jump from our stairs onto a big beanbag chair below. I can proudly state that our home now has a "No jumping from higher than the fourth step" rule. However, give him a blanket or a box and he will slide down the entire flight of stairs.

Needless to say, he doesn't fit into the mold that schools love, and even as hard as he tries, he struggles with sitting still and doing tedious, or, as he calls them, boring tasks. His desk has an elastic band at the bottom where he can pretend to "run" while sitting. At his parent-teacher conference, his teacher told me she was worried he might actually be the first student to wear out the band. I thought, *Yep, that's my Elijah.*

In spite of his fearlessness, the swimming pool was his nemesis.

The home we rent is part of a homeowner association, which means we pay fees so we can have flowers at the entryway and deal with someone measuring our grass length with rulers, but as a reward, we have access to a spectacular swimming pool complex. This club has two pools, a waterslide, a splash pad, and a kiddie pool. I love that my kids get the experience of swimming on a regular basis, especially having moved from Minnesota, where summer is often a mere six weeks.

But our first summer there, none of my little boys could swim yet, including that superfearless *American Ninja Warrior* hopeful of mine.

Lack of swimming skills didn't stop us from going to the pool, though. When we first started going, Elijah and his little brother, Samuel, would get in the three-foot-six-inch section and cling to the edge. Not only would they cling there, but they'd also barely move from the safety of the steps, where they could easily climb out.

As the summer nights rolled by, they both began to find their bravery and slowly started venturing further into the pool without the known safety of the wall. You could see how proud they were, those almost-swimming kids with their new courage. After a month of frequenting the pool and watching all the other kids jump in, Elijah determined he, too, was going to be a jumper. I mean, seriously, how could he not? Kids were doing cannonballs all around him. And he's a risk taker. Risk takers don't watch; they do.

That mindset, *I'm going to jump into the pool,* changed one night. While I was swimming in the middle of the pool with Samuel, I glanced over to the side and spotted Elijah standing at the edge, looking like he was actually going to jump in. Prior to that I had been asking him about jumping, but the more I asked, the more he hesitated. At some point I stopped urging him to jump, because I realized he was going to do it when he was ready. Bravery in life—whether it's jumping or doing something else—has to come from within oneself.

That night in June he looked different.

He looked determined.

I could see it immediately, in the way we moms just know, and I realized he was trying to find the inner bravery to jump without me directly below him. I'm sure that for the risk-taker boy, having his mom standing in the water below yelling "Jump! I've got you!" was a lesson in humility. I knew he didn't want me there, but for those previous weeks, he either watched or needed me, not jumping on his own.

But now the risk taker was confronting his fear and letting bravery rise.

I stayed back, not wanting to disrupt his brave self, and as I watched, I saw him move his lips and count, "One, two, three . . ." Then he'd bend his legs deeply, and when he said "three," instead of doing an uninhibited, fearless jump, he'd catch himself and stay right there, standing on the edge of the pool, his toes still gripping the concrete. Over and over he'd count to three, squat, almost jump, and remain stuck.

"Elijah, what's going on?" I asked him as I swam closer.

"My legs want to jump, Mom, but my mind keeps stopping me," was his frustrated reply.

My mind keeps stopping me.

Elijah desperately wanted to jump because that fearless, adventuresome part of his heart was pushing him to try. However, his brain, the logical self, was still afraid. I kept giving him reasons that he would survive the jump, trying to minimize his fear. I showed him the lifeguard three feet from us, then the one across the pool. I splashed the water around me and reminded him I was there in the pool waiting and wasn't going to let him drown. I gave him all the reasons that he would survive it.

But no matter how much truth I told him, he still was the only one who could overcome his own fear. It wasn't my voice that would shut out the worry; it was only his. *He* had to decide to jump.

WHAT'S STOPPING YOU?

That jumping struggle? It's universal. I can easily identify with Elijah's internal battle. I mean, half this book is my sharing with you how I got stuck, gripping the edge of my life in fear of what would or wouldn't happen. When I first took swimming lessons, I stubbornly sat on the edge of the pool for eight weeks while my mom, bless her heart, watched and probably hoped from the bleachers that I would get in. Every week she'd encourage me to try, and every week, on the edge, I would remain dry, letting my fear override expectations. My irrational fear allowed me to be frozen, not caring that my mom paid for lessons, that I was the only kid who sat on the side (while still wearing the swimming cap that never touched water), and that I was making a scene. It took eight weeks at those beginning lessons before I even ventured into the water. No one pushed me in, no one lowered me in, but it took *me,* in one moment when bravery spoke louder than fear, to have the courage to actually climb down the ladder and into the pool.

Making changes is a balance between the brain and heart, a tension between the risks and the practicality of logic. Logic tells us to stay safe, gives us reasons why jumping isn't ideal, tells us to jump tomorrow, when conditions might be better, and even tells us we don't need to jump.

The heart is love, daring, free, and exhilarated at jumping.

The brain is rules, expectations, mortgages, and warnings.

On that hot summer night in the pool, I stared my Elijah in the eyes and said, "Elijah, deep down your brain wants you to jump but is nervous about what happens *after* you jump. It's worried about water in your eyes and mouth and nose and if you can pop up quickly enough. That's okay. It's all right to have those worries. But *now* I want you to tell your brain a new thing. Tell your brain your heart wants to feel the water on your face and to feel the awesomeness as your feet hit the water. Tell your brain it is okay to jump. You will be okay. And, Elijah, I absolutely know you will love it."

"You think so, Mom?" he asked hopefully.

"I know so."

Now I could see it: for the split second that counted, he believed me. He had hope, and with that hope his risk-taking bravery was given permission to speak louder than all the fears. He counted again, bent those legs, and gave a hop, and this time on three his toes released their grip and his body freely jumped into the water.

"You were right! You were right! I can do it! It's totally awesome!" he shouted after he swam to the edge. His face was beaming with joy, with pride, with accomplishment. He smiled at me, climbed out, walked to the edge that had once held him back, looked at the pool, and then instead of going through the process, instead of doubting, just jumped.

He jumped again and again and again.

Each jump brought more joy, more risks, more excitement.

What he feared became what he loved.

It's easy to tell someone, "Just jump—you'll be fine," and get exasperated when she appears to stay standing at the sidelines of her life. In the beginning, I was frustrated that Elijah wouldn't just jump, because I *knew* he would think it was exhilarating. But expressing frustration to someone who is stuck means we forget what it's like to be stuck.

When we're stuck, it doesn't mean we don't know we need to jump. It's rather we don't know the path or even what we're supposed to be jumping into, and that fear of the "what happens after" keeps us counting, "One, two, three," over and over and never leaping.

Fear is a stifling voice of the unknown.

It takes self-confidence to muster the courage to unearth the fears holding you back. It takes faith to examine the fears and replace the fallacy of most fears with truth. Elijah's fear of the water was based on facts. People do drown in pools, do hit their heads, don't like water in their eyes. But despite those being facts, the potential of them becoming a reality was distorted. He needed to understand that the .00029 (or whatever number it was) percent chance that his fears would be recognized was not worth overriding the 99.99971 percent chance that he would love (and survive) the jump. This doesn't mean we jump without thinking. The brain is powerful, and fear is not always negative. Through trial and error, you've learned not to touch the stove, because now you fear the blistering burn if you put your hand on the burner. Fear of the hot stove saves you from pain.

But on the flip side, our brains can remind us of failures from twenty years ago and turn them into current, and still painful, holding-us-back facts. They have the ability to bring up times when we fell and attach to them the warning of "Remember the last time you followed your heart and how that hurt?" Having hopes dashed—just like for Joseph, for me, for many of us—is painful, and when risk is linked to the potential of pain, it's easy to allow that fear-stopping power to have control over us. Who wants to get hurt? To fail? To fall down? I avoid those if possible.

But sometimes that's exactly when you need to examine the fear your brain has linked to alleged outcomes. If every time you get determined to jump, your brain screams, *Warning! Warning! Warning!,* as if you're going to touch the stove, then of course it seems safer, more logical, to avoid the pain.

CONSIDER WHICH WARNING IT IS

What if the warning was wrong? Have you thought about that?

The reason it's hard to challenge fear is because fear's emotional response on our bodies is great. In fact, the response—increased heart rate, anxiousness, fast breathing—can be so uncomfortable that it makes it challenging to dismantle the *why* behind the fear. Let's imagine that in seventh grade you totally bombed speaking in front of the entire school and everyone snickered. Now fast-forward to the PTA president at your kid's school asking you to speak in front of the group about some policy change, and you without thinking respond, "Oh no, not me. I'm not good at public speaking." Are you really not good at public speaking? Or have you believed the agreement, based on past results, and never challenged the belief about your ability to speak in front of other people since seventh grade?

Challenging the belief, deciphering the root of fear, doesn't mean you stand up to speak in front of a thousand people tomorrow. Challenging the belief means you are willing to understand why you are afraid, why you dismissed the opportunity, and not just accepting that fear is a reason to not try. And many times you don't stop to figure out *Why did I just say I was not good at public speaking?* but rather just accept what you reason and tell others as ultimate truth.

So how do we decide when our brains are legitimately helping us and when they are just getting in the way, most often listening to past paradigms and fears?

If I asked you if the seventh graders who laughed at you should help you determine which school to send your kids to or what mortgage company is the best today, you'd probably chuckle and completely disregard their authority to assist you in making a current decision. Yet the fear still linked from them to public speaking potentially stopped you from saying yes to the PTA-meeting opportunity. The power comes when you ask yourself why you respond to certain situations with words of perceived truth.

You can overwrite fears and attach the appropriate warning to legitimate ones.

Elijah needed me, his truth teller, to give him enough logic, enough fact, so he could have faith in his heart's desire to jump. In reality, he didn't just ignore fear; he reasoned with it and won with truth. At some point, whether he realized it or not, he began to fear not jumping in the pool and missing out *more than* all the worries he had about what could happen if he jumped.

The fears of losing my house, losing my kids, not having enough food, not being happy, getting to the end of my days with a list of things I had hoped to do but never did—those became more important to me than my fear of letting others see the real me behind the masks. The warning for fear shifted from fearing change to fearing doing nothing.

You have the power to lead your thoughts to new truths, to new logic, to new mindsets.

You can use fear to your advantage.

Isn't it time you stopped wishing things would change or wondering who you are and took control of the fear stopping you? I don't think there are many eighty-year-old grandmas sitting around high-fiving each other for all the times they did nothing and just wished things would be better. In fact, I once listened to a TEDx Talk from a first responder to critical accidents, and he said that of the people who later died, they shared with him three common things. One of those? They regretted not taking the risks.

In order to change, you need to stop fearing the change but instead fear the results of *not* trying to change. What happens if you don't jump? What happens if you stay where you are right now? Isn't the greatest risk the risk of doing nothing?

Exist or risk. Dream or do.

Fear not changing, and you will change your life. Take your dreams, the places where you have never jumped, and ask yourself, *When I'm eighty, will I have jumped?* Then ask yourself, *How will it feel if when I'm eighty I never mustered the courage to jump?* I think you'll get your answer about what you need to do.

The straight-in-your-face truth (just like my counselor, Ed, gave) is this: if you start changing now, you're one step closer to it no longer being a fear but instead a jumping fact, a story you will tell about the time you confronted fear and won.

Make the Jump

You can't jump unless you know that you need to.

Elijah knew the pool was his place for change. I knew writing and providing money was a space I wanted to change. Others want to learn to play guitar or sing in church. It's great to want to jump, but you must want to complete the jump.

And that means you need an end date.

Without a date, the dream is simply a nebulous maybe, a possibility. With a clear end date, you set into motion the wheels of the universe, of your mindset, of others helping support that deadline.

At a blogging conference I helped coordinate, I had the privilege of meeting and chatting with Michael Hyatt, an author I admire. After he spoke to the group, I grabbed my copy of his book *Platform*,[4] which he'd autographed at a different conference, and when the crowd cleared, I walked up to him, thanked him again, and asked him to re-autograph it. Everyone laughed at my need for the second autograph. My blogging friend Jenn piped up and told him how I wanted to write a book. He looked up and asked me about it and why I hadn't done it. I gave him the deer-in-the-headlights look and tried to come up with a reason, but it didn't matter.

He opened my copy of his book, found a place to sign it *again*, paused, and wrote, "Get it done. No excuses! I'm counting on you."

As he handed it to me, he looked me in the eyes and said, "And so is everyone else."

End of the story? Nope. His agent saw what he wrote and followed me into the other room. I told him how I was so blessed by Michael's words and that I was going to write a book now. But he told me, "That's not enough. You need to write down your end date. When are you going to have it done?" He wasn't going to let the moment pass. Instead, he pulled out his phone, turned on the video recorder, and filmed me telling him and Michael the end date.

Accountability.

This was not what I was expecting. Stating the goal was almost easy. Setting an end date for the goal was terrifying because once I decided on the end, it set into motion the chain of actions to get there. It made me accountable to a dream spoken. Beyond that, because there was a date, I was now in the position of either finishing by the date, or never attempting it and knowing I quit on myself.

The date I decided on was August 2, 2013. Exactly six months later.

I wrote. And wrote. And on August 1, 2013, I sent Michael a note telling him I'd finished writing my book, *Dear Mom Letters*.

He replied, "I always knew you would."

Don't worry—we can hone in on the dream. We can figure it out. What matters most is that you decide a date in your future when you are going to see actual change.

You need to come up with a date to finish your dreams. The next sections in this book are written under the assumption that you have a dream—something you want to start/stop, something you want to do—coupled with an end date. And, friend, for you it might not be a dream like starting a business but rather fixing places in your life, as I had to. But you need to choose a date. Maybe it is a date three months from now when you are going to realize a big dream. Maybe it is the date when you want to start classes. Maybe you want to buy a house or go on a trip.

You are going to come up with excuses.

Don't worry about those. Don't listen to the voice of fear of the unknown and let that override the bravery it takes to write the end date. This is the moment when you get to decide your path.

You must have a date you want this done, completed.

This is the big risk. Know your jump.

Keep it in your head and you risk it staying there. Write it down and you risk it happening.

Which risk are you going to take?

Part 2

EXPOSING EXCUSES

Carry on, brave mother.
Carry on, brave mother who tries when she's
      tired.
Carry on, brave mother who gives
      unconditionally.
Carry on, brave mother who cries because
      she loves.
Carry on, brave mother who hopes without
      answers.
Carry on, brave mother who loves without
      expectations.
Carry on, brave mother.
Carry on.

—Rachel Marie Martin

Why don't you just jump?

It's not that easy, right? If it were, the pool of opportunity would be full of adventuresome souls constantly accomplishing crazy things.

The truth is most everyone aches to jump at some point in life. We possess Elijah's desire, but something holds us still. For years I'd look up to all the jumpers, wondering why in the world that wasn't me. I also know that for years I held on to dreams I wanted to accomplish and problems I wanted to fix, yet often despite my best efforts I ended up not moving, not jumping at all.

Imagine it this way: it was as if I had one foot on the accelerator without realizing my other foot was pressing down equally hard on the brake. No matter how much I tried, as long as I held a foot on the brake, I wasn't moving.

These are the excuses, the brakes in life.

Excuses is a loaded word, isn't it? Especially for moms. How many times do we teach our kids to go above and beyond and to stop using excuses to get out of their responsibilities? The mere thought that we somehow conjure up excuses to avoid doing something is almost against the universally known and unbreakable maxim called Mom Law. We're not the excuse conjurers; we're the moms, the excuse busters. We're the ones in the pool explaining over and over why the jump will be awesome.

Despite our diligence in dismantling and seeing our children's excuses, we aren't as diligent about getting rid of our own. We don't grow up and grow out of excuses. Now, being a busy mom can seem like a valid reason not to change. So can existing in a messy life. Or having no money. Or having a challenging marriage. Or being a single mom. Most of the time we mask our excuses as noble reasons *not* to do something. But we must understand deep in our hearts that those excuses are the ones that will subtly keep us surviving throughout our lives without ever moving inches forward.

Until we deal with the mindset of excuses, we can't even go to the practical steps of how to change in order to more fully pursue and realize our dreams and who we were created to be. So let me be the voice that tells you to *knock it off* and take your foot off the brake. You can't justify your excuses, because your justifications are just as virtuous as "My dog ate my homework." We're just smarter, more sophisticated in how we rationalize our excuses as legitimate reasons to stop pursuing change.

Remember Steve Miller's advice on time?

Excuses or not, your life will tick by. And all that stuff you are going to write down and figure out how to do? You *must* find a way to do those things, and you *must* decide that accomplishing them is more important than the excuses that stop you.

I know we use excuses because they seem acceptable. But when it comes right down to it, they are all just defenses. We can't change or move forward until we face them straight on. Listen, you are going to have part of you that says, *Nope, not me. I don't have any excuses.* Expect that, okay? But the second you start to dismiss an excuse is the second I want you to wonder, *Is it possible I'm using that excuse?* Be diligent and seek out the defenses.

Just so you know, there are three main types of excuses: denials, baggage, and agendas. I'm going to go over each type, break it down, and help you see the areas in life where the excuses in each category may keep you stuck.

Don't run from this. Embrace it knowing that every single time you dismantle the excuse, you are lifting your foot off the intentional or unintentional brakes in your life.

8

The Denials

There was a day when I looked in my bathroom mirror and didn't recognize the eyes staring back at me. I remember the water splotches on the mirror, the new wrinkles on my forehead, the towels on the floor. But my eyes? The loss of self? I didn't want to see that part. Looking away felt easier, felt safer, felt right.

There are spaces in our lives where we cannot ignore what's reflected back. Choosing to mutter "It's no big deal" or "I'm fine" is choosing to stay stuck. Don't self-sabotage, thinking you don't have any denial excuses. In fact, if you're thinking you'll just skip this section, chances are you're noticing the towels on the floor and not the reflection in the mirror begging you to take back your life.

Denial will keep you not only in the dark but also viciously stuck.

THE EXCUSE OF IF/THEN

From the time we are little, we have dreams. If you have forgotten this, just go sit around little kids as they talk about what they want to be or do when they become grown-ups. Those six-year-olds will tell you with unshakable confidence that someday they are going to be doctors or travel to the moon. They don't have any excuses for why their dreams won't happen.

As we get older and the burdens and expectations become heavier, we begin to qualify and deny the validity of the dreams we have. Now our dreams have practical parameters attached to them. In my life, even in the years when the finances limited the options, I always wanted to write, to speak, to travel the world, to go on mission trips, to help people. But because I believed I was stuck, I told myself (and others) I could do those things *after* everything keeping me stuck was fixed or when the kids were grown. My excuse?

If the money situation were fixed, *then* I could help others.

This is the subtle excuse of if/then.

If/then thinking is deciding not to move because we assume the "then" happening is a prerequisite to action. We believe that results cannot be pursued until we are in the "then" space of our timeline. The danger of this excuse? You deny any responsibility regarding your influence in the very current "if" places of life.

When you accept, *If this will happen, then . . .* , you are actually stating, *If this happens to me, then . . .* You are not saying, *When I get this done, then . . .* , or *Despite the obstacles, I'm going to pursue the "then" I always wanted.*

Would you play the lottery with your life? Betting on a hypothetical future before you make a change? At a deep level, if/then is gambling with your future. Sprinkle in some entitlement, for those who expect the "then" to just show up, and it's like playing the lottery but expecting someone else to buy the ticket.

Look at these other if/then excuses I've used in my life:

- *If* I could keep the house clean, *then* I could be happy.
- *If* I had an extra hour in the day, *then* I could take time for myself.
- *If* I had money, *then* I could start to blog.
- *If* I weren't afraid of rejection, *then* I could get that job.

Here's the blunt truth: We can help others whether we have billions of dollars or none. We can be happy whether the house is spotless or a pigsty. We can take time for ourselves whether we have an extra hour or an extra five minutes. We can blog whether our checkbook has excess or none. We can apply for that job whether our application gets accepted or rejected.

Do you realize the "then" is your dream? Look at my list again: help others, be happy, take time for myself, start to blog, get that job. All the items immediately following the "if" were my excuses, the brakes of if/then that kept me from chasing the dream.

If we always delegate the "if" to someone or something else, we're refusing to take charge of our own futures. It's easy to sit with friends and discuss all the "then" places in life. What if you decided to be the friend who looks at your friend and tells her to stop basing her future on the "if"? What if you had the wild abandonment of your six-year-old heart again?

If you decide to wait, *then* what happens?

THE EXCUSE OF GRATITUDE

I am a grateful person. Being grateful is an easy—and important—thing for me to do. I taught myself gratitude as an antidote to the hard stuff, and being intentionally and authentically grateful has brought me needed joy. This is important because joy is independent of circumstances and involves my heart posture being open to good despite the circumstances.

When I first started blogging every Friday, I hosted a post inviting readers to share their favorite things from the week. I'd write about how I was thankful for the warm coffee cup in my hands, the sun sparkling in the windows, the gluten-free bread, friends who called, a garage to store my things (the irony). *Finding Joy* became a collection of joy-filled moments in the midst of an unsettled and challenging life.

Despite my intentional and rightly ordered gratitude, I was also grateful for the places that needed to be changed. In other words, I tried to find silver linings around spaces that really just needed to be fixed. I became nobly grateful in the hard places. Instead of facing them head on and working to change them, I disguised denial as gratitude and used that as my excuse.

Soon that kind of silver-lining gratitude became my drug.

Just as a drug numbs pain, being perpetually grateful despite terribly hard things excused me from taking action to fix the hard places.

Here's an example of how I used gratitude as an excuse. One December day many years ago after returning from that lost dream job in San Diego, I opened the shades in my Minnesota living room and looked outside at the freshly fallen snow covering my driveway. It was beautiful the way the snow blanketed everything, covering the trees and leaving the world looking white. But as I admired the view, I also started to get uneasy—something seemed wrong. I studied the scene harder, trying to shake that feeling, and in that moment, I realized our gray two-seater Toyota Tacoma—which we had purchased in California and which had been sitting in the driveway the night before—was gone.

Now shaking, I walked outside and looked around, just in case someone had moved it and I had just missed it from my living room glance. I hadn't missed it. It was simply gone.

Vanished.

As I stood in the snow, the reality of the moment began to creep into my heart. The truck wasn't accidentally missing—it was intentionally removed. I had seen the late notices in the mail, added them to an unopened pile on the desk, watched them get buried.

I knew. It was repossessed.

The freshly fallen snow eerily covered the tracks of it being taken in the middle of the night. As the world awoke to the beauty of the new snow, the ugliness of my day hit deep, and bitter tears stung the corners of my eyes. The thought of people sneaking around on my property, removing the truck, while my little kids slept in their bedrooms, was enough to fuel deep anger. I felt violated.

I felt helpless too—incredibly helpless. I wasn't working, I had a new baby, and now random people were granted the right to step into the sanctuary of my home, even if only outside, and remove the masks of outer perfection I desperately didn't want others to see. Having a truck disappear isn't an easy thing to ignore.

"Why?" I cried. "Why, God? What am I doing wrong? I'm trying so hard! Why do you let this keep happening? Why? Do I not matter?"

Then I heard a knock on the large front window. My little kids, looking out the window, thrilled about the new snow, were waving to me with excitement. They were innocent, little, and not needing the burden of knowing why the truck was no longer in our driveway. As I looked at them, I transformed the furious lines on my forehead into the "It's no big deal" smile moms give when we protect our young.

Now, here is where the gratitude excuse entered. This experience should have been a sign to me to change things, especially with those little kids in my care, and make sure it never happened again (which it actually did). Instead, because I felt as though I was without options, that I wasn't good enough, and I didn't think I knew what to do, I took the anger and fear and spun them into gratitude.

Later that day, after we tracked down the truck at a repo lot, we were allowed one trip to the truck to gather our personal belongings still inside. You want to know my response? I actually said, "I'm so grateful we can get our stuff out of the truck at the repo lot. Thank goodness. What a blessing."

Was that really a blessing? One could argue that it was, but only if getting a truck repossessed was out of one's control. My not being the provider didn't exempt me from deciding that looking away wasn't an appropriate solution. At a certain point, I needed to expose the stack of bills, not allow them, and seek out help. But in the days that followed, when others asked about the now-missing truck, I made up a story about how our situation wasn't fair and it was unexpected that we lost it. Instead of being truthful about not making our payments, instead of asking for advice on how to confront this issue, I played the passive role, hoping and praying for good results despite no effort and dealing with being knocked down by covering it with gratitude.

I don't know why no one said, "Knock off being grateful that you can get your stuff out of your truck that you clearly stopped paying for. You need to stop denying responsibility and fix this. Let me watch your kids for you." But they didn't. That's the reason I'm telling you that it's possible to use gratitude as an excuse. My gratitude hid the seriousness of my life, my passivity, and my fears.

Yes, I *am* genuinely grateful I was able to get my stuff out of the truck on that winter day, but when I used that to excuse and dilute responsibility, I was demeaning and twisting what gratitude actually is and does. And worse, I used it to not change and to deny seeing reality.

Inauthentic gratitude—the kind of Pollyannaish idea that everything is rainbows and unicorns when your world is falling down around you—shifts the focus from fixing the root of the problem to blurring the effects. Think about this. Rather than being grateful for everything others gave us—my parents buying our house, my parents giving us their old vehicles when ours broke, friends paying for Christmas presents and soccer lessons for our sons, the church buying us food over and over, the church buying us a microwave and dishwasher, the loans never repaid, and on and on—and using that gratitude to move us forward, at a certain point all that gratitude without action pivoted to entitlement.

How shallow did my gratitude sound to my parents, who paid the mortgage on the house every month and gave us a new car? How honoring was that to them?

We become entitled when we are grateful for other's solutions to problems that we could be active in fixing ourselves. Financial problems happen. But sitting around, praying without action, and not being active in finding new jobs, dealing with creditors, and fixing the mindset that leads to losing jobs is not rightly ordered.

My gratitude for the results of passivity became more important than kick-starting the bravery to no longer accept the results of the problems as acceptable and right.

Instead of being "grateful," the way to honor yourself and those in your life is to pick up the shovel, call the creditors, face the friend, deal with whatever you are accepting, and start doing the work to change it and your mindset. This is not easy, because it means debunking your own excuses and admitting that you have been hiding.

Be grateful always. But remember that true gratitude compels you to take action, to change, to be thankful, to be purposeful. Inauthentic, entitled gratitude, however, distorts capabilities and responsibilities and gives permission to remain stuck. Don't allow *that* kind of gratitude to cover up the need for action.

Look at your gratitude list with a critical eye and ask yourself if you are being grateful for places of stuck that actually should be places of change.

Don't deny yourself from seeing the places of needed action.

THE EXCUSE OF ROLE

From an early age we're assigned roles: hall monitors, lunch-line captains, student council presidents, shift leaders, camp counselors, resident assistants, and more. We give our kids and ourselves roles that define responsibility even further, such as using chore charts and assigning who's in charge while we walk to the neighbor's house and whose job it is to get the mail. Roles become even more defined in the workplace, where we're given a name tag, a business card, an office title, and a path of roles to get a promotion.

Roles don't disappear as we age. In marriage (and relationships) there is often an invisible division of labor that develops. It's an efficient way to divide responsibilities between two living in the same space. One person may be the only one who trims the kids' nails, while the other always takes out the trash. Some roles are defined mutually, others by external forces. You may be the one to wake up early and get the kids ready for school because your husband's the one who works third shift and gets home at 2 a.m. That's a role given due to circumstances.

For the most part, roles provide order and a means to organize tasks. For example, the shift leader at Starbucks is there to ensure that orders are met, cups are stocked, the store is clean, and customers are happy. But sometimes in relationships (or life), we use those roles as excuses.

Note that roles should never be confused with basic responsibility. As parents, we have the responsibility to raise our kids, feed them, provide a home, keep them safe, and help mold them to be upstanding citizens. This is not debatable.

In my marriage, I was clearly given the role of homemaker and educator, not breadwinner. For more than fifteen years, I allowed my role to stop me from fixing our family's deepening financial problems. When I attempted to make changes, ask questions, and take on even the smallest part of the financial role, I was reminded that was not my role. Instead of it being a mutual space of growth and responsibility, it became an isolated space of anger, passivity, and rebuke.

The hard truth was this: our bills needed to be opened, employment was required, the IRS should have been paid, our reliable transportation should not have been taken overnight, and I should not have had to rely on friends, family, and church for food long term.

Based solely on an assigned role, I denied myself the power to change something.

My kids also did not deserve their mom crying on the doorstep, helpless in her role, as she figured out how to tell them the truck was gone. They, too, deserved a rightly ordered life.

That meant that despite the roles we started with, at a certain point I needed to remain homemaker and assume responsibilities as bread-winner as well. Someone needed to stop the cycle. It was imperative that I carefully and critically examined the roles I had accepted in my life. Maybe you do too. Do you dismiss yourself from change, responsibility, and choice due to a role you've adopted, accepted, or been assigned?

What changes need to be made in your life that you've been turning away from because of a role? Could you take over the finances? What about making that suggestion to your boss at work despite it not being in your wheelhouse? Could you find a way to volunteer even though your plate is full? Do you accept the age you are as a limiting factor?

Roles are great. Roles unchecked can become excuses.

Do you risk disrupting comfort in an attempt to take back the spaces in life that are neglected? Do you risk challenging the status quo and decide to pursue greatness?

In the true story of Erin Brockovich, this single mom didn't allow her lack of education, money, and business knowledge to stop her from securing a job at a law firm during her family's financial crisis. Once there, she didn't let her role as assistant keep her from digging deep and uncovering critical details in a health lawsuit. She went on to be a key player in a class-action lawsuit, helping dozens of families. Because she didn't let her role limit her, she went on to change not only her life but also the lives of thousands.

Don't ever let a role excuse you from taking responsibility.

THE EXCUSE OF PRACTICALITY

There is an agreement our culture has made with all of us regarding the "good" life. The good life, whether articulated or not, goes like this: be a good kid, graduate from high school, go to college knowing what you want to do, graduate, meet someone, get married, get a good job that pays the bills, have kids (but not too many), get a house with a double garage, coach soccer, put the kids in school, volunteer, get a bigger house, sing in the choir, go to Disneyland, deal with the teen years, graduate the kids, downsize the house, become grandparents, vacation, retire.

At funerals, we often hear a person's loved ones say, "She had a good life. She was blessed." It's the unspoken goal. We reinforce it in our teens when we ask them, "So what do you want to study in college?" as though that is the most practical step on the good-life path. We reinforce it in one another in many ways, from the expectations we see on Pinterest to the pressures of making sure our kids get into the right preschools to the way I hid the interior of my home behind a perfect good-life white front porch.

Practicality keeps many of us stuck chasing a path that few actually get to walk. I didn't follow all the "good life" steps—sometimes by choice, other times by consequence—yet I felt I deserved the comfort that comes with always taking the practical path. I didn't want to break the illusion of not having it all.

My friend Peter appears to have it all: a beautiful house on several acres, three kids, a wonderful wife, a fantastic and desired job, tons of money, a retirement plan, exotic vacations. He is the epitome of sensible, the poster child of society's good life. Yet recently he told me how for the past twenty years, he gradually became numb to his own heart. He's a deep thinker, a dreamer, a family man, yet he admitted how he lost himself in the pursuit of the prescribed practical path.

Remember, on the outside, Peter looks as though he has everything.

He doesn't have to work to hold up the masks of the good life as I did, yet his good life has left him feeling just as hollow, just as trapped, and wondering if his heart and dreams will ever have a spot of priority again.

He had written down dreams—scratched them on paper, hoped to pursue them—but lost them as his timeline of years ticked by while he kept busy, kept working, kept doing what was expected. Somehow his need to fulfill the good life placed his once-powerful dream list in a new agreement we make as adults: that dreams are impractical.

Some of us exist in a comfortable place, a drama-free normal, yet we still have those moments when we realize that in the midst of the good life, we've forgotten our hearts' callings. Peter even attached the word *youthful* to his current dreams.

The quickest way to deny dreams of our hearts is to describe them as silly whims of youth.

Does fulfilling your dreams have the potential to disrupt your current comfortable? Can you hear yourself excusing them away as not fitting into today's timeline? Peter was hesitant to change his job, to alter his focus, because he and his family had grown comfortable with the money and lifestyle the money afforded. And beyond that, he didn't like sharing with his support group of friends his "youthful" dreams. He feared they might look at him differently, might think he was in the midst of a midlife crisis, and that meant uncomfortably revealing that his good life wasn't all it seemed.

When we put our desires and dreams on the shelf because they might receive the "foolish" label for breaking the status quo, we use practicality and comfort as excuses for denying dreams. Does keeping up with the Joneses trump change? When we are old, which will matter more: that we stayed practical or that we pushed ourselves out of comfort?

Comfort can also come in discomfort, although few of us would ever admit that. There are many times when I look back at my life and wonder why I didn't change things more quickly. Change is difficult, and the fear of the unknown brings with it discomfort. So many times, it becomes easier to remain in a comfortable discomfort than taking the risk on the comfort that comes with nontraditional dream chasing.

I know you are not reading this book to stay in your normal and never change. You're not reading it to figure out how to make the perfect pot roast with the roasting pan you have tucked in the back of the pantry. You're not reading it to be told a whole bunch of cheers about why life is perfect right now and to be convinced that you should just smile and push forward. I hope you are reading this book to rediscover yourself, to fight for your heart, and to live with deep joy in the midst of motherhood. That means you cannot hold on to comfort as your excuse for not being brave and moving forward.

Getting comfortable in our own lives—whether it's the good life or a normal life or a messed-up life—allows for complacency and tolerance.

Practicality is easy to tolerate.

You survived yesterday, so as long as you don't change anything, you can probably survive today. But that is why you are here now, in this place, reading this book, wondering who you are or daring to dream, probably after hundreds of days of comfort. I'm here to tell you that there's comfort on the other side too—the side where you're longing to be happy again. What about the side where you're pursuing dreams and pushing the envelope? There's comfort over there too. Why live away your life in restless comfort, when all you have to do is decide you want a better, more fulfilling, higher-level normal? And you know what? Every day you risk, you open your days to tremendous awesomeness. You will meet new people, discover your strength, laugh more, and in it all know that at the end of your life you can say, "Thank goodness I took that risk."

Otherwise you could live your life in practicality but always think, *I wonder what could have happened.*

THE EXCUSE OF SCARCITY

For twelve years I homeschooled my children. During those years, I never wanted to part with the textbooks I taught from, for fear we wouldn't have the money to get updated ones. Even after I wasn't homeschooling, I held on to those books, thinking I could eventually sell them. I had an entire ten-foot-long and three-foot-deep shelf in my garage stacked with homeschool books (remember the jam-packed garage?). I had them organized and bundled neatly together, yet despite this, they were getting more and more outdated every day as they sat there waiting for me to sell them.

At one point several years after my divorce, when I began confronting excuses, I also started cleaning out my garage. I easily got rid of many things, drove to the dump I could now afford to use, and donated items. But those treasured homeschooling books? They sat on that giant shelf, boxed up, staring at me every time I went into the garage.

Have you ever held on to items because you feared not being able to replace them? I knew I couldn't keep those books. I knew they were weighing me down. I also knew I would potentially be moving in the next year, and I didn't want to drag those heavy boxes with me. One spring-cleaning day, as I stood there in the garage, I came face to face with a debilitating excuse.

I had believed in scarcity more than abundance.

The opposite of living out of scarcity is living out of abundance. Living out of abundance doesn't mean living foolishly. It doesn't mean sitting back hoping great things will happen. It means that when you wake up, you see possibility and potential and then act and live as if you have enough now.

Scarcity believing means you assume that if you don't have enough now, you won't have enough in the future. It closes you off to options, makes you cling to things too tightly, prevents you from taking risks. To live with an abundance mentality means you see what *could* happen, independent of money and where you are now.

Before I took control of my financial life, I would have been angry if anyone told me I was using money as an excuse not to pursue options in my life. The lack of money limited my ability to see potential and stifled creativity. Our dismal finances became the excuse that stopped me from daring to embrace possibilities.

Ironically, I didn't allow scarcity to limit my kids. Because my kids were homeschooled, I wanted them to be a part of a community of home-school kids. I found a co-op that met once a week, and for five years, we were part of an amazing group of families. Did I have the tuition? Nope. But I put myself on the line, humbled my pride, did the work I needed to do. Beyond generous partial scholarships, they were able to attend classes because I showed up, negotiated remaining fees, volunteered, and did what it took to ensure they could learn art, music, and science. I refused to allow my financial lack to ripple into their opportunities. It was humbling indeed, but they were worth the fight.

But my own change? My own desire to take piano lessons again? To find ways to speak to others? To go on that mission trip? For my own dreams, I permitted the fear of scarcity to be my limiting agent. All those homeschool books gathering dust on a garage shelf represented potential income, yet because of the fear of letting go, they sat there, unused, really being a physical representation of scarcity's grip.

Despite my bills all being paid now and debts being dealt with, I still catch myself (and my kids because of having heard me for so long) making scarcity statements. Sometimes one of us will say, "It will never happen because it's too expensive." In that moment, I stop, break down the scarcity principle, and illustrate how the word *never* limits possibility. *Never* and *always* are universal qualifiers in language. There are few opportunities and places that you and I can *never* do something. (For instance, I will never be able to play basketball like Michael Jordan. I will never be able to sing like Adele. Or another truth, there will never be a day when taxes are outlawed.) Yet we sprinkle *never* and *always* through our thoughts freely. Scarcity is living with thoughts that claim, *There will never be enough money* or *I'll never have an opportunity to make it back* or *I'll always be broke.*

To break scarcity, you need to live out of abundance.

Actor and comedian Jim Carrey is said to have written himself a $10 million check years before he received his million dollars for acting in *Ace Ventura: Pet Detective.* Elvis was told to go back to Memphis and become a truck driver. Socrates was told he was an immoral corrupter of youth. Lucille Ball's drama teacher told her to try a new profession. J. K. Rowling was rejected by more than twelve publishers before the first Harry Potter book was sold. None of these people lived thinking that scarcity was in their future. They had unwavering faith in their dreams and gifts, and because of that vision, they operated out of an abundance posture of living.

Using scarcity as an excuse to stifle movement is a subset of the first denial excuse of if/then. Have you ever told yourself that if you had more money, *then* you could take that class? Or travel? Or fix things? Or be happy? Allowing money to be the final determiner of potential shuts down your abundance mindset.

For years I wanted to blog, to write, but I thought to get started I needed money to design the perfect website. One day eight years ago, I realized that my life was ticking by and that if I always waited for enough money, I might never write. In the moment of realization, I broke my own excuse. I found a free platform, used a template as a design, and started. It wasn't perfect, but it worked *and* it didn't cost money.

As I continued to write, I continued to claim a life of abundance, opportunity, and potential, and soon I began *making* money off my blogging. Then I published my first e-book, which provided even more money. Then I took another risk—one that scarcity would have shut down—and asked a big company to sponsor and send me to a blogging conference where I could learn even more about this craft. Even though I couldn't afford to go, I decided to live out of abundance and simply ask. When I emailed the company, I didn't ask as though I were expecting no for an answer. Instead, I presented a confident woman, having faith that the future for her didn't match the amount in her checkbook.

Oreck, the first company that believed in me, said yes. They covered airfare, hotel, conference admission, and even extra expenses.

In that place of abundance, I learned even more how to live a life of abundance. To live out of abundance, you need to dismantle scarcity thoughts and not be afraid of the potential no you may get in asking.

Our financial disaster was never out of my potential control to re-solve it, nor did God turn a blind eye to the situation. It did mean that I didn't look away, didn't run, didn't hide. I chose to believe, despite having a checkbook with little in it, that much would be provided. But it wouldn't be provided by sitting still. It took belief coupled with daily action to roll the snowball of abundance forward.

Instead of using scarcity to instantly answer your dreams with why it won't work, change your thinking to abundance and figure out *how* to make it work.

How can you attack the situation you are in? How can you start that class? How can you begin to write? How can you pay off the creditor? How can you volunteer?

You know *why* you want to, so now don't deny yourself the oppor-tunity of *how*.

9

The Baggage

The second category of excuses is made up of the ones that weigh us down. On *The Biggest Loser,* a reality show sharing contestants' massive weight-loss journeys at a fitness ranch, there comes an anticipated day late in each season when the remaining contestants run a race. They start the race with weights strapped to them equaling their starting weight when they arrived months earlier. As they run, they reach milestones representing each week, where they unstrap the amount of weight they lost for the particular week. At each checkpoint, with the bags of weights dropped, the contestants' speed picks up from barely a walk to a full-fledged run.

They start burdened and always cross the finish line feeling free.

Almost every season the contestants remark how they astonishingly didn't realize how much the excess weight was holding them down when they were overweight. Yet months later, when they were strapped up with the "lost" weight, it felt oppressive. As they physically dropped the weights, they share with the viewers a powerful example of how we can be held back without realizing all we carry.

The baggage excuses are the same. We don't automatically pick up a ton of weight and decide to run life's race with it, but rather over the course of time this baggage accumulates. It is the slow, often imperceptible toleration of more baggage that slows us down and oftentimes absolves us from action.

These are those excuses.

THE EXCUSE OF GUILT

It doesn't seem to matter what I write on my blog about breaking through and living to the fullest. Inevitably at least one mom will reply, "Oh, but I feel so much mom guilt." Once she writes those words, she opens a tidal wave of other moms joining in, sharing their own stories and struggles with mom guilt. We all joke about this hidden guilt and chuckle about its power, yet the reality of its hold, its weight, on our lives is prominent.

Have you ever spent time focusing on yourself and it felt great, but you still had that little voice questioning if you really should have taken that time? Mom guilt makes us question ourselves, makes us excuse ourselves from doing things we desire because we feel the need to redirect our focus on details that aren't as urgent. Taking care of our kids is incredibly important, but if you experience guilt for taking care of yourself while taking care of your kids, you might be dealing with unhealthy and stifling mom guilt.

Think about this. If you've made an agreement with yourself that good moms stay at home, you've created a culture around you that promotes your staying at home. If you desire to return to work, you first have to untether yourself—and those around you—from the "good moms stay at home" agreement and recognize that you are still a good mom if you work outside the home.

But that also means you will change the comfort dynamics for everybody involved. Even the smallest, simplest change, such as taking an art class on Wednesday nights with a friend, may come with dinner groans, bedtime complaints, and laundry cries. The pressure can come from yourself as you deal with your own monologue of guilt. Don't discount mom guilt, because that subtle guilt, that "I'm not a good mom if I do this" worry, can pull you astonishingly fast back into being stuck and deciding not to change.

The decision to attend an art class on Wednesday nights might mean saying no to the playgroup and moms club you organized and are in charge of on Thursday mornings. It might mean looking for someone to take care of your kids during those hours so you have time for the class. It might mean having to deal with friends who think you are a hypocrite because you were the mom who said she'd never put her kids in daycare. It might mean acknowledging your own previous opinions about daycare and babysitters. It might mean letting go of fear.

The first time I left my kids to attend a blogging conference I wrestled with deep mom guilt. As I was seated on the airplane, waiting to take off, I surprisingly struggled with enjoying the freedom I felt—freedom because for ten years prior, I had never had a night away from my kids. I was always there, always home, always giving. And now, here I was seated in a window seat, watching the world become smaller, and I felt happy to be away from the kids and responsibility. And that happiness, that freedom, stirred in me a bit of guilt. I questioned why I felt guilty for taking a break and why I thought previously that if I were a good mom, I wouldn't need a break.

You won't find me telling you not to take a break. In fact, I want you to take breaks. Motherhood is an exhausting journey, and you need to be responsible for yourself as well. You cannot give if you are empty. There is nothing wrong with needing, wanting, and appreciating a break. Taking time for yourself isn't indicative of lack of capability but rather is important for fueling self.

But guilt's weight? It whispers to us, *You are not enough.*

When you hear those qualifying words, it is your responsibility to decide not to carry them. We moms tend to judge our own capabilities by comparing our lives with those around us. If our friends change, guilt wants us to think that we, too, need to change, because we must be dropping the ball somewhere. Listen, every one of us has a different path, different talents, different gifts, different dreams. You are enough when you follow yours and love your friends for following theirs. Releasing comparison will help you let go of the excuse of guilt.

If you are juggling all the things mom guilt makes you think you should be doing, you will not have time to let some of the balls drop so you can find yourself again. Because in truth, you *can* take an art class on Wednesday nights. You are a good mom if you teach the family to support you, to support one another, to become a two-way street of support. Being a mom doesn't mean that you forget yourself.

When my daughter Grace turned driving age, she was excited to learn to drive. I was terrified but knew that riding in the van with her while she learned (with my foot pounding the imaginary brake on my side) was part of the process. I had to consistently remind her not to stare right at the pavement in front of the hood but to gaze farther down the road. When she kept her eyes low and focused on the next ten feet, she was constantly course correcting, making micromovements of the steering wheel. As soon as she had the confidence to look up and down the road, her grip on the wheel loosened and she could focus on driving, not correcting. Guilt, especially in the "I should be doing more" arena, is like course correcting everything. Grace was going to make it to her destination either way, but the course-correcting way was exhausting and stressful.

Your kids will grow up. You will make it through these years, but you need to decide if you're going to listen to guilt's loud voice or look up and not allow guilt to weigh down your decisions and outlook.

The best way I've found to confront mom guilt is to remind myself to breathe. Guilt chokes out the oxygen in your life because you spend all your time making sure everyone else is breathing and you forget to take your own breaths. Remember, if you burn out, you can't mother anyway. If you're going to feel guilty, feel it for *not* taking care of your heart and dreams, because denying self leads to burnout.

Your kids need you. Your heart needs you too.

Look up. The future is full of possibility.

THE EXCUSE OF PRIDE

Remember my overpacked garage? Remember how I refused to let people enter my house? So much of that was because of pride. I was afraid of what people would think about the real me. Pride can convince us to hang on when we really need to let go. Letting go isn't failing, yet pride loves to make us think it is. Is it really an accomplishment to be the last one standing if it's in a place we shouldn't have remained?

Pride makes change challenging because it values current self-image more than the process of future change. Pride tells us:

- What will people think if I try and I fail?
- They don't understand my problems. I'm different.
- I need to make sure I look like everyone else so no one thinks I don't have it together.
- I can do this all by myself. I don't need help.
- I don't need to understand the steps. I already know how to do this.
- That job? I'm too smart to take a job like that.
- Who do they think they are to criticize me? They obviously can't see.
- It's hard to change when nobody notices and tells me they're proud of me.

Pride is the opposite of rose-colored glasses. Instead of seeing possibilities, it filters every result, every solution, every problem, every change through self-image. Pride is a stubborn excuse.

Look again at the list of ways pride stops us and the antidote we need:

- **What will people think if I try and I fail?** So what if you try and fail? Do other people have authority to define self and success? Do you think *other* people never fail? Everyone has failed at some point doing something. The best chefs have failed. The greatest actors have failed. Writers have failed. Speakers have choked. It's a natural part of life that is meant to teach us, if we will let it.

- **They don't understand my problems. I'm different.** This is ego driven. We all have problems and trials, and discounting the advice and wisdom of someone else because you have determined that your problems are unique will shut down the creative and collective forces of community working for change.

- **I need to make sure I look like everyone else so no one thinks I don't have it together.** Again, pride's ego. Sometimes this world needs more moments of tears around the Bible study table, where we don't have it together. When we drop our masks and let ourselves be real, it is often the best time for change because instead of chasing perfection, we can chase change.

- **I can do this all by myself. I don't need help.** We all have shortcomings and places where we need help. I'm still not the best at getting rid of things because I have emotional attachments to stuff, so, as you know, my stuff tends to grow. However, when I allow my friends to come in and stand in the gap and help me get rid of excess, they open the door for me to experience change. Help is good.

- **I don't need to understand the steps. I already know how to do this.** No one is born understanding calculus. I couldn't play Mozart on the piano until I learned to read notes, practiced scales, and put many hours into understanding and learning. Not giving yourself grace to go through the steps means you'll get frustrated before you start. This is like expecting to shoot every free throw perfectly without ever having picked up a ball.

- **That job? I'm too smart to take a job like that.** This implies a level of inferiority thinking that you have regarding everyone else. When there are needs and jobs, sometimes we have to humble ourselves and do the hard things so we open up for good things. Dismissing an opportunity as below ourselves shuts down opportunities. Don't let ego trump the actual steps in life. When I was in Haiti, there was never a place of ego regarding intellect and work. Work was a gift to be taken and never was linked to smarts.

- **Who do they think they are to criticize me? They obviously can't see.** Ego again, and it can make you quit because your pride won't allow you to receive criticism, even if it might be helpful and beneficial. And so what? What if you *are* criticized? Does that mean you stop moving forward? What if the individual has a point that could make you a better person? Don't be so quick to discount someone else's comments and insights. When I was in college, I studied architecture and design. As part of the process, our artwork had to be taped to the walls and then critiqued by the class. I quickly learned that those who grew were those who weren't offended by the evaluation but rather were grateful another set of eyes saw something they had missed.

- **It's hard to change when nobody notices and tells me they're proud of me.** What if no one ever says anything to you about your massive change in life? Does it make your change any less powerful, important, and profound? You don't need outer validation to approve heart movement. Being told that you do amazing things or that someone is proud of you is wonderful, but don't rely on accolades to propel you forward.

Be on the alert for the ways pride can get hold of your bravery and ability to move forward. Pride is a subtle excuse, but the effects are powerful. There is great freedom in not allowing the weight of pride to mask the real you. When I finally removed pride's baggage and shared with the world my broken places, it was not met with pity but with love. And beyond love, my willingness to be honest motivated others to be honest and brought many people into my life who said, "You are not alone." Don't listen to pride's lie that you'll be alone if you are real. Instead, have confidence in me and know that letting go of pride will bring opportunity, friendship, and fresh perspective.

THE EXCUSE OF WORRY

Just as I was born with the extrasensitivity gene, I also have a quadruple dose of the infamous worry gene. I'm sure my parents will gladly verify the truth of my worrying tendencies. In fact, I can't remember a time when I didn't worry about something. I probably worried I wasn't a good baby or didn't crawl quickly enough. I know I worried about my appearance or if I was a good enough mom. Worry is a superpower that's not so mighty, cloaked behind my very adult way of saying, "I'm just analyzing and assessing the situation."

My dad called me out on that when I was young. And last month as well.

And dozens and dozens of other times. Even that worries me.
This past week alone I worried about

- my kids taking the bus
- my kids forgetting the card I wrote their bus number on,
  which, by the way, was the third card I made
- my second grader's shoes coming untied, because he's not
  great at tying
- me not being a good mom because he can't tie his shoes yet
- money
- my hair falling out
- my anemia
- my weight
- still not being a good mom
- money, again
- one of my daughters not having a good day
- what to make for dinner
- the gratitude section that I deleted twice in fear of what you
  might think
- losing some of the good words in the delete, which I now
  can't get back
- sharing too much about my life in this book
- not sharing enough about my life in this book
- you thinking I worry too much

I have a worry addiction.

I need to be clear: worrying and analyzing are not the same thing.
When you analyze something, you identify the problem and put together
a written plan of solution and then action steps. Worry is when you identify the problem and obsess over it and don't move on to the solution or
action.

Worry will never change a situation. I have experienced dozens of occasions when I wasted time worrying about something that resulted in nothing. I frustrated my friends with my doubts, pestered many with questions, spent numerous hours fretting, only to discover there was no problem. All worry does is rob you of your time *before* the situation, so you actually suffer twice. I've suffered many "twice" moments in my life, and because of my worry excuse, I need to call us all out on that tendency to sink into worry.

If you are a worrier, you are not alone. You and I could be part of the Worry of the Month club easily. However, you need to examine your worries and determine if they're moving you forward or just creating a spinning cycle of immobility and procrastination. Worry is the ultimate stopping weight of carrying the burdens of indecisiveness, *What could happen?*, and fear.

To quiet worry, you need to confront it. Start by writing down your concerns. Put a notebook by your bed, use a voice recorder, anything. Get them all out. If you feel a worry arise, add it to the list. Don't judge it—just write. But don't worry then about what you just wrote. Instead, set aside time each day when you allow yourself to worry. During your allotted ten minutes or so, don't question yourself or fret—just be free to worry. But when the timer dings, you're done. Then take your worry list and analyze it. If you can change the thing you were worrying about, then, well, you have your new to-do list. If you cannot, then let yourself worry for a second more, and then you must let it go. Otherwise it will become baggage.

And I mean let it go. I recently saw a new counselor who realized I spent considerable mental energy worrying about situations that ultimately didn't matter. She then told me that in life we should have our moments when we have an exuberant yes or an equally exuberant no. Everything else in between is not worth hanging on to and mulling over. To let go of worry, we must have our definitive yes and no places. The rest we cannot carry. My simple visualization for releasing worry? I imagine the remaining worries as the white fuzz on a dandelion that's gone to seed. And then, in a moment of personal power, I blow that fuzz, those worries, away. Once worry is released, the power for it to occupy our minds is also released.

This simple practice has moved the nebulous, happen-any-time baggage excuse of worry into a focused, get-it-over-with, find-resolution freedom.

THE EXCUSE OF EMOTIONAL BONDS

I hate to admit that I've held grudges, but I have. And they are crippling. Holding a grudge against someone you live near means worrying about seeing him or her at the grocery store, avoiding certain restaurants, choosing not to attend meetings, staying inside when you know the person is driving by. It can be an excuse not to get that job, volunteer, or help because the grudge is thicker than the freedom. Do you have that person? That person who when you find out he or she is coming, you decide to not go? That's the limiting weight of emotional baggage—it is an excuse to not do something based on a noncognitive response.

Holding a grudge also means limiting opportunities based on some circumstance that happened in the past. I have known families in which the siblings didn't talk to each other for forty years because of *one* incident in the past. And then instead of harnessing positive energy and good memories of the life before the event, all they do is cling to the grudge, to the perceived power in clinging on to something that should be let go of. They don't allow themselves a future with healing, just pain from a moment.

Holding grudges is like living in a dungeon without doors. Keeping the pain hostage while waiting for the person to show signs of remorse and guilt doesn't serve anyone—especially yourself. Maybe you want to volunteer at school but stubbornly hold a grudge against the PTA president, so instead of giving time you stay home out of spite.

What is a grudge keeping you from experiencing?

No one binds you to a grudge except you. You can't expect progress if you're unwilling to budge.

Emotional baggage does nothing but tear at your heart. It eats up precious moments, and it stops you from pursuing things that could positively bring you joy. And although the distance of time only makes it harder to forgive and move on, it is forgiveness that opens the door. Forgiveness doesn't just benefit the other person; it also frees your spirit.

Don't wait for an apology. You owe it to yourself to let go before the grudge turns into bitterness.

Emotional baggage isn't limited to just grudges either. We can have such strong emotional bonds to things that we can never let go. Staying in a 2,200-square-foot house because you need the storage for 124 boxes of stuff you can't live without means you can't quit your job and take a lower-paying one, because then you wouldn't be able to make the mortgage payment. It also means that to live in that downtown loft you just adore, you'd have to work more to pay for the storage unit.

Several years ago on my blog, I started a tidying challenge inspired by Marie Kondo's book *The Life-Changing Magic of Tidying Up*. Kondo challenges us to go through every single item and ask if each one sparks joy in our lives.[5] As I began to let go of the items in my household, I was shocked at the emotional baggage I'd attached to my stuff (beyond scarcity thinking). Some of it was pure sentiment. I was saving many things I assumed mattered to my kids, but I discovered they could not have cared less about them.

I had a box filled with American Girl dolls my daughters had received as Christmas presents from their grandparents. I was convinced they would want those expensive dolls and dresses and the memories attached to them, so I tucked them in a box, thinking they were priceless. When I asked my now almost-grown daughters about them, expecting to keep the box in storage, one of them nonchalantly said, "You can sell them or give them away. I really don't care."

It was another box of stuff that had my emotions attached. It was another thing to be managed.

When we keep stuff, such as those American Girl dolls or the artwork or the baby shoes or whatever, we are potentially attaching emotional baggage not only to ourselves but also to our kids. The second we pass that box to them labeled Memories from Childhood, we've created an emotional link for them, which might cause them to think, *I can't throw this away because Mom saved it for me.* Now our excuses are passed down to them.

When you have less stuff, you create freedom and space within your life. Once I got rid of my stuff, eliminated the emotional attachments, I found myself in a home with 80 percent less stuff. The garage was empty, with bare shelves. One night after the last boxes were hauled away, I was playing in the backyard with my two little boys and felt a freedom I'd not felt in years. I no longer had the constant nagging thought of *Shouldn't I be cleaning the garage?*

Finally, I had margin, where I could choose to spend time doing something I desired without the guilt of needing to manage things in my home. And in that moment, I wanted to be spending time with my boys. And the feeling of freedom was so surprising that it still makes me smile.

Examine your home. Take a long hard look. What if you lost everything? Tornado. Fire. Flood. What would you actually miss? And what are you managing? What are you clinging to because of the emotional lure? Do you spend time maintaining, as I did? Are you hanging on to stuff?

My garage may have been full, but none of that stuff in there filled me with happiness. If you aren't using something now, you'll never miss it. There are things we can save, for sure. Pictures can be digitized. Home movies can be uploaded to a computer. And do you really need *every* piece of your child's third-grade homework? Maybe you can just pick out a couple of things that fit in the scrapbook. Or better yet, take a picture of them. Simplifying creates freedom.

The baggage from the past doesn't need to define a moment of the future. Until you can release yourself from the bond of emotional baggage, you'll put off finishing priorities in the name of managing and taking care of your baggage. It's an excuse that's stopping you from spending time on things that matter.

It's okay to let it go.

By the way, it's been two years since I purged my house, and the only things I have found myself missing are the piano books that I'd used for teaching, which I had initially held on to, thinking that my kids would use them. I didn't realize I missed them until my son Caleb asked for a book. In that moment, I knew I let them go. But that didn't matter because instead of worrying about replacing the book, I got in my van, drove to the music store, and bought him the book he needed.

Letting go didn't mean I never had the book again. Letting go meant I got rid of the books we didn't need in that moment and had the space to buy the exact one needed at the right time.

And as far as releasing grudges? I like my freedom now.

Don't let the baggage excuses weigh you down.

You deserve to run.

10

The Agendas

Some excuses can make us feel extremely productive. Who doesn't want to get stuff done? In fact, we exist in a culture that praises productivity. Just today, as I stretched my almost healed ankle in physical therapy, my therapist asked, "What are your plans for the weekend?" Even though it's just a conversation starter, there is the underlying idea that we must have some sort of agenda, something we are doing. But sometimes the agenda we think is ideal and correct can be an excuse with a mask that stops us from doing what we need to do.

The agendas—the excuses in this final section—often collaborate and work together, so if you find yourself identifying with one, be prepared, because one of the others might be adding fuel to your excuse fire.

THE EXCUSE OF BUSY

Sweet Grandpa Witt, my mom's dad, was a farmer in southern Minnesota. During harvest time when I was a little girl, my folks would pack up my siblings and me and we'd drive down to his farm for a visit. During the day we'd play in the kitchen, while Grandma and my mom prepared meals for those in the field. We always slept in the room above the front porch, and often throughout the night I heard the workers come in and out, in and out. Yet I didn't see my grandpa much during harvest.

He was in the fields.

He was not in the barn organizing shelves. He wasn't sweeping the stable floor eight times a day and rearranging the hay in the loft. And he wasn't polishing the tractor's attachments, despite his love of his John Deeres. He was putting his energy where he needed to expend it: on the harvest. He may have been busy, but his busy was focused, rightly ordered.

His busy was for a set time and a specific result.

My grandfather would not have said yes to the kids if they wanted to go to Disneyland during the harvest. He would have told them no sleepovers, no Chuck E. Cheese's parties, no karate lessons if he had to be the one to shuttle them. Sometimes taking care of the harvest means all the distractions must be put on hold because that one thing is more important.

Grandpa Witt taught me an essential lesson during his busy season: when it is harvest time, you focus on the harvest, not on the barn.

I will never ever say that motherhood lacks an element of busy, because I've been constantly busy being a mom for the past twenty-two years. We moms are always busy doing, managing, working, negotiating, cleaning, dealing, and mothering. Whether we are toting around multiple kids to numerous events or handling the mess in the garage or in the yard or in the laundry room or picking up toys or washing dishes or rearranging books or volunteering or cleaning or re-sorting toys or using Solomon's wisdom to break up today's important battle of who gets the computer first, we are there, creating order, making meals, answering emails, trying to remember to breathe, being told we should rest, all while trying to exist on scant amounts of sleep until busy starts again.

Out of breath? Yes, me too.

Motherhood is without question one of the busiest times of life. We will *always* have one more thing to do, one more load to wash, one more closet to clean, one more mirror to shine, one more homework sheet to check. But there are times when we need to remember that we should be harvesting, not maintaining.

Here is how busy is an excuse: it gives a false illusion of control. During the years when my outer world was filled with chaos and hardship, I felt without control, without options. Staying busy let me avoid stepping into the messy, needing-change portions of my life—from being audited by the IRS to struggling through a failing marriage. But it also kept me from pursuing my brave side, the side that grasps for the inches of change. I didn't really spend time in spaces where things would change; I just rearranged the spaces of my life to create a semblance of order and temporary accomplishment. In other words, to use my grandpa's work ethic as an example, I was tidying the barn when I should have been in the field.

The brake of busy prioritizes nonessential items with greater importance and dilutes the critical importance of essential, life-changing action. There is a profound difference in doing what needs to be done immediately versus doing what can be done tomorrow.

In the book *Breaking Busy*,[6] my friend Alli Worthington details how being busy gives her a rush of accomplishment—I can relate to that—but also keeps her from looking at the corners of her life that she has been neglecting.

You must understand that when I was busy, I felt good, as though I were fixing things that needed to be done, thus that rush. But I was ignoring what needed to be done. All busy does is rearrange the current without influencing the future.

In order to break out of the busy excuse, you have to stop what you're doing and ask yourself *why* you're doing it right now. What's the point of organizing the silverware drawer? Is it something you would *like* to have done or something you *need* to have done? Are you organizing it so you can put off doing something else? Is it critical that you devote time to volunteering, or is it better to say no so you can work on your goals? If you have ever thought, *I wish I had an extra hour every week,* and you're also the person alphabetizing your cereals, then you, my friend, might be using the excuse of busy.

You will be busy. I can guarantee that.

But make sure that in that agenda, some of your busy is time devoted to the busyness of *change.*

That is *real accomplishment.*

THE EXCUSE OF PERFECTIONISM

There are times when I'm at the store and I'll see a mom chasing a rambunctious toddler girl. The mom will seem frazzled and I'll think, *I bet that girl is a Grace.* And more times than not, I'll hear that mom yell, "Grace! Stop! Grace!"

I know this phenomenon because I have my own vivacious daughter Grace. When she was little, she had no problem telling me her opinions and she also had no problem stating them in front of everyone. One day we were shopping and as we walked by the lingerie section, she asked about why it was on display. I whispered to her that it was the underwear section. That spunky four-year-old child walked next to me for the next ten minutes with this perplexed look, and then seconds before we were to check out, she stopped and yelled, "Oh, I get it! That store part is private, right? Like butts-and-penises private?"

I was mortified. She was sincere. She didn't care what people thought; she just wanted to know why there was an underwear section at Target. She's my Grace.

Grace is about living fully: she doesn't need to get everything "right" or perfect. Grace will come home from school and tell me how a 93 percent A is just as good as a 99 percent A at the end of the year. She can see the A and is content, whereas I am a die-hard perfectionist. I see the 93 percent and dwell on that missing 7 percent. That's what perfectionism does: it keeps us stuck or at least chasing points that ultimately don't change the final outcome.

Too often we don't change because we spend so much time trying to get step one perfect that we never get to steps two, three, four, and five. Or we don't appreciate the end because we discount the steps we thought we completed in between.

Prior to my divorce, most nights we ate meals around the table. I loved dinnertime, even with the stress, because it was that moment of good. It was a gratitude place indeed. In the first weeks after my divorce, though, it was painful for the kids to see the dining room table incomplete. But my 99 percent A, perfectionist self still fought for meals around the table. This resulted in a great deal of frustration and tantrums from all of us.

The truth is that I was aiming for a reality that in that time needed to be reevaluated and let go. I couldn't move forward because I was clinging to the expectation of "*This* is what we do." It was my friend Dan who alerted me to my own perfectionism. He heard me being hard on myself and lamenting my failing dinnertimes. Without joining in the lament, he simply said, "What if you put dinner on your island, called the kids, let them get it, and then cleaned it up forty-five minutes later? Bless them with a space to grieve instead of forcing 'family dinner' on them."

He was right. Rather than seeing the greater good, I saw the articles I read on the importance of family dinners. I didn't see my kids' hearts. Dan saw that I wasn't giving myself grace because my perfectionism clouded my perspective.

I stepped back. I made dinner and sat at the table. Those who ate with me ate with me. Sometimes I ate alone, and instead of feeling sadness, I prided myself on trying. As time went by, the family dinner morphed and gradually returned to table gathering. Releasing my perceived perfect created an atmosphere of healing and new beginning.

Maybe this was a season when I earned an F for family dinners around the table, but once I let go of the need to recreate what once was, I got an A for looking after my kids' hearts. It's impossible to live with everything perfect, as there is a give and take and ebb and flow of time that needs our attention. Good moms don't always have family dinners. Good moms listen to the needs of their families. Good moms see the power of showing up in the imperfect perfection.

Perfectionism stalls change's momentum. It partners often with busy and worry because we could always be busy making everything perfect or worrying about how it isn't. But the perfection is often reserved for the outside of our lives, not the inside, not where change needs to take place. Change is messy, the antithesis of perfection. Yet when change is fulfilled, it is exquisite. We cannot fight the messy parts of change either; we cannot force it along.

As difficult as it is to let go of worry and perfectionism, remember that grace is on the other side. Just the other day my now-seventeen-year-old Grace sent me a text. We all were in our respective bedrooms because I'd had a hard day and blew up, telling the kids how all I did was mess up and that nothing I did mattered. Her text simply said, "Thanks, Mom, for taking me to Target and buying me gummy worms. You're a great mom. Want a green one?"

Grace from Grace.

She didn't see the stumbles; she didn't care about the 7 percent where I thought I'd failed; she loved the 93 percent where I tried my best. When you battle perfection, you need to step back and say, "Does it need to be absolutely perfect for me to move on?" and chances are you will see you can take the next step much more quickly than you previously thought.

Give yourself the gift of grace. The perfect agenda doesn't dictate success.

THE EXCUSE OF PROCRASTINATION

Several years ago, the world was introduced to a seventeen-year-old sage named Zach Sobiech. I first saw him on the local news in Minneapolis, and as the year progressed, I learned more about his story—his pivot place in life. His pivot wasn't a mindset choice but a reality choice, and it came in the crushing diagnosis of terminal cancer. From the moment he found out this information, he made powerful decisions every day about his now clearly finite life. Unlike most of us, he was given a general end date for his earthly existence. Because Zach could see this date, it gave him a new hierarchy for life, which allowed him to understand he could either live with joy or live with bitterness. He could make a difference or fade away. He could speak truth or stay quiet.

SoulPancake, a YouTube channel highlighting stories of hope, featured Zach's story and his quest to share his perspective on mortality with those whose lives weren't clearly marked with an end date. He lived his last year, as poet and philosopher Henry David Thoreau described and Zach often proclaimed, wanting "to live deep and suck out all the marrow of life."[7] He recorded songs, dreamed with wild passion, and spoke wisdom that outlived him.

In the video, Zach eloquently noted, "I think every teenager out there feels invincible. And they'll never admit it. It's not the kind of invincible like Superman. It's the kind of invincible like 'I'll see you in five months.' I thought I was invincible. I was ready for college pretty much, and I was planning out way ahead. Then, yeah, it turns out sometimes you can't do that."[8]

So often we think we're invincible. We tell our friends, "Let's get coffee on Tuesday after Bible study," with confidence that Tuesday will come. Instead of living in the tension of the timeline, the ticking of the years, we ignore the finite and live believing we have forever, or at least many years ahead of us.

I actually think I'll live to be eighty-two and sit around in the retirement facility, talking with my friends about our lives. I imagine I'll be joking about those floral-pants days, sharing about my travels, and boasting about my grandkids. That means, in my believing-I'm-invincible story, somewhere in my heart I truly anticipate and expect forty years left of my life. But that also means I have lived more than half my life; I have used up all those inches of time. Yet somehow I can still convince myself to rest in the presupposition that I have time left to do what I need and want. Because of that infinite time, I give myself permission to put off doing what's important. Do you know what that putting off is?

Procrastination.

It's the killer of our dreams and the crusher of our bravery. But what makes us procrastinate?

When I was young, I'd come home from school on a Friday afternoon with a backpack bursting with homework. I'd drop the backpack on the floor and proceed to do other things. My dad would take one look at the backpack and push me to do my homework right away. Being a procrastinator, I would hold off. Despite my being the worrier, it took a while before I worried about the bursting backpack.

The next morning, I'd watch Saturday morning cartoons—loved those eighties Smurfs—then play in the afternoon, master a level on the Nintendo video games, and try not to think about that homework, especially when I saw the backpack sitting there untouched.

On Sunday I'd go to church and later watch football with my folks. Then by five o'clock, there I was, exactly where I was Friday, with a giant bag of homework just waiting to be opened.

"If you'd just do the hard stuff first, Rachel, then you would be free to enjoy your weekend versus always knowing you have homework to do," my dad would say.

My dad is wise. He's an engineer and spent his life developing systems and processes. He also knew that I had to feel the regret, the pressure, the angst of not doing the hard stuff a couple of weekends before he could teach me the lesson of priorities.

Even if you avoid what you need to do, there will still come a day when what you've been avoiding becomes unavoidable. The homework wasn't going to magically get done. It took only several weeks of staying up, sitting at the table, desperately trying to write those papers, before I decided to heed my dad's wisdom. Dreams don't magically happen because they are dreams. We're not entitled to have them come true, nor are we entitled to have the issues that we *must* rightly order in our lives be resolved without effort.

Be brave. Think about the things you want to complete, and identify the hardest, scariest thing that's keeping you from accomplishing them. Look at your worry list for inspiration. If you haven't written down the steps you need to take because you'd rather avoid that scary thing, be even braver and decide to write them down or jump in and start. That is what Zach Sobiech would want you to learn; that's what became urgent to him when he saw his own finite days. That scariest item is your number one priority. Make the call, type the email, clean the toilet, register for the class, put on the running shoes, whatever it may be.

Do not make your agenda wait until tomorrow.

If you can stop thinking you can do it tomorrow and instead live like you should always be making progress today, you'll achieve your dreams. I have no doubt. The reward comes when you start crossing off things from your list that don't keep your foot on the excuses brake, and that alone will move you forward. Even if it's just an inch forward, it's movement.

One final thought: if you tell yourself, *I'll get to that [whatever your dream may be] when the kids are older,* then you believe you are invincible. Whatever you're putting off in the middle of motherhood, write it down and start working toward it today. I've had too many friends who have had their lives cut short to know that I'm not invincible. I am sure you also have had that happen to friends. The best way to honor their legacies is to stop living as a slave to procrastination and bite the bullet and try.

Your kids are only young once.

You're only the age you are right now once as well.

Remember Grandpa Witt? Every season he planted seeds, anticipating a harvest. He didn't allow any excuses to keep him from doing what he was called to do. His pride didn't stop him from getting help. He didn't let worry about rain coming stop him from planting. He didn't carry emotional baggage. He didn't allow scarcity, despite living during the Great Depression, to slow him down.

My grandpa put all the seeds in the ground, believing in the harvest. Even though he believed, it didn't mean there were years when the harvest went perfectly, when there wasn't fatigue, when there wasn't worry, when there wasn't waiting, when there wasn't work. He always took the risk and planted dry corn seeds into the earth in anticipation of the harvest.

Remember, it's about the harvest, not the excuses. My grandfather didn't permit a single excuse to keep him from *harvesting* the corn either. He knew he had a window of time in which to devote his energy and resources to gathering the abundance of what he'd planted. That corn wasn't going to stay ripe forever.

Your task? To be aware of the excuses you give yourself. Your reality won't change if you allow excuses to be the brakes. Dare to lift your foot from the brake.

Have faith. Put in the effort. Release the excuses and run toward your harvest.

Part 3

BUILDING A NEW REALITY

Today is not defined by the past.
It is your clean slate, your start.
Be fearless and tomorrow will be different.

—Rachel Marie Martin

Dear Sweet, Sometimes Not So Sweet, Kids of Mine,

There's something you need to understand.

I want you to know how hard I try.

I really need you to know that. More than anything. I haven't been perfect. I've messed up more times than I can count, I've lost my cool, but in it all, I've really tried.

There are so many nights when I go to bed and I cry.

I think I've failed.

I worry that I've let you down. I see the promises I didn't keep or the things I didn't do. I see all that stuff that messed up the perfect plan I had for your childhood. I didn't want you to have to deal with the heartache of divorce or seeing me work super hard.

I wanted it to look different.

But despite all that, I try. I want you to have a life of joy, of opportunity.

That's why I try.

It's such a heart try. I tried the day the first one of you came home and I looked at your little face, not having a clue what to do next. Just because I didn't have a clue didn't mean I stayed stuck. Instead, I tried. I figured out how to feed you and change you all. I figured out bedtime and snack time. I figured out the doctor visits and memorized the doctor's office phone number. I figured out preschool and kindergarten and grade school and middle school and high school and college.

Just because I didn't know what to do next didn't mean I stopped.

I kept going.

Year after year.

Making birthday cake after birthday cake, wrapping present after present, paying bill after bill, driving to lesson after lesson, saying prayer after prayer.

Because more than anything, my trying is from this deep love.

I'm never going to be perfect. And neither are you. I'm so glad you got to see me stumble so much, because in every single stumble of mine, you didn't see me stay stuck—you saw me try again.

We tried.

Despite our messes, we created a story, a family, an adventure, your childhood.

It might never look like a Hallmark movie, but oh my word, it is our story. I'm so proud to be your mom—beyond proud. There are nights when I look at you sleeping, and tears well in my eyes, and despite the slammed doors and late homework and "I hate you" moments, all I can feel inside is the deep love of motherhood.

I love being your imperfect mom.

I'll never stop trying. Never.

I'll move forward, fighting.

If anything, in all these years, that is what I want you to know.

I tried so hard because I love you so much.

Thanks for trying with me. Thanks for loving me. Be brave, be bold,
and love others.

And always try.

—*Me*

(Written to my children in the middle of my harvest years.)

11

Break the Cycle

I learned to hate the sound of knocking at my door. Years past, a knock typically meant someone was bringing trouble, not friendship. And because I rarely allowed anyone into my space and life, knocking immediately made the hair on the back of my neck stand up straight and my pulse quicken.

One spring day, when the checkbook was more negative than positive, when my youngest child still fit snuggly on my hip, the dreaded knock came again. I cringed, fearing it was the mail carrier bearing yet another overdue notice for me to sign, but this time as I spied through the peephole, I saw a very large man with a pipe wrench in his hand. I didn't want to be the one to deal with this, but I was without options and home alone, so instead I put on my sweetest smile, tucked Samuel in tighter, opened the door, and kindly said with a wavering voice, "Hello, sir."

I attempted to charm him with sweetness, a baby in my arms, and pleasantries.

He, despite my best efforts, wasn't there to be kind. He was there to turn off the gas.

He had an exceptionally booming bass voice, and the quieter I spoke, the louder his voice became. Right about then my other kids came running upstairs, drawn by curiosity brought on by the doorbell. "Mom, Mom, who's at the door?"

I didn't want them to know why he was there. I didn't want them to bear the burden and fears of poverty. I needed them to see me as strong, despite the helplessness inside, because I was the person who was supposed to protect them. I shooed them outside the back door to play.

Despite my outward attempts at coolness, my legs didn't play along with the hide. They were shaking, and that shake was making it up to my hands. I was terrified. In those scrambling moments, I desperately tried to figure out how to stop this man from walking the fifteen feet to the side of my house and turning off our gas. Unlike with the repo day years earlier, this time I was face to face with the person who was going to alter the uncomfortable normal I was protecting.

"Sir, would you mind coming inside so I can talk to you?"

I was so afraid of him exposing my world to the outside, my neighbors across the street and the kids who made their way playing to the front, that I was willing to expose the inside of my world, the Legos all over the floor, the dishes piled in the sink, the couch without the throw blanket covering the rip. I don't know if he had compassion or not, but for a moment he hesitated and looked at me with kindness. That simple moment in which I was a person, not just a problem, gave me strength and courage.

But then he proceeded to tell me that it was against policy for him to enter my home. However, he did lower his voice as he said, "I need you to come up with $914 immediately or I am required to turn off your gas."

To be transparent, in those days, that amount of money felt insurmountable. I wasn't working, was raising the kids, and rarely could venture into the store to purchase what was needed. One humbling time, I sat in a grocery store parking lot counting out change to buy a bag of frozen corn, crying as I scrounged around for the eleven cents that I was short. So $914? Back then I really didn't know what to do.

And then to add to the moment's drama, right on cue, my Samuel started to cry.

"Shhh, shhh, shhh," I desperately urged as I rocked him back and forth and back and forth. The rocking was for my heart too. This was a cycle in my life. It kept happening, this repeat of someone coming into my space needing money that was rightfully theirs. I hated it more than anything, hated those knocks, hated the fear, hated the shame, but it all kept happening.

Now, I don't want to air all the details of my marriage, but I need you to understand that at some point I had to make a choice to look at the cycle of poverty, late bills, and passivity that kept spinning and decide that if action was going to be taken, then it was my responsibility to do so despite roles. For me, taking action also meant that the good-life illusion came crashing down, and fighting for the kids and myself meant ending a dysfunctional cycle and exposing to the world my true story.

My life's timeline had a cycle embedded within it. We all have these cycles in some form. However, for us to break free and move forward into the brave life, we must unearth those cycles that hold us back and keep us spinning and then *do* something about them.

THE LIFE CYCLES THAT KEEP US STUCK

Cycles happen everywhere.

Think about it. There's the water cycle (in which precipitation and evaporation go around and around), the rock cycle, the moon cycle (with all its phases), the planetary cycle, the nitrogen cycle, and more. The world is full of spin.

The timeline of our lives doesn't always move forward linearly. Sometimes there are cycles stuck within our years. Here's how they spin:

We spent the first section of this book talking about agreements. Those are the spaces where we have accepted truth about our future and potential. Those agreements fuel excuses. As a result, the excuses solidify the reality or current situation we are in. While time keeps progressing forward, the patterns of time continue to endlessly loop.

In my case, the reality of the knocks, collection notices, and judgments came so frequently that I began to believe with finality that things would never get better. This became my agreement; the knocks became about worth, not change. As a result, I convinced myself I was powerless and unable to resolve the finances. I used the excuse of role as my validation not to step in and take the steps to fix the reality, which then strengthened my agreement about worth. Then when the next knock came at the door, I "proved" the cycle. Proving it doesn't change it but instead allows it to repeat.

The thing about these cycles we get stuck in is this: we give the habitual excuses that we aren't capable of stopping them, that we need another person to save us, that it's someone else's fault we are even there, and that we don't have time or energy to change.

In my life, the more knocks, the more I was knocked down. The more I was knocked down, the more I doubted change. The more I doubted change, the more I accepted the cycle I was caught in as a law of life versus a variable that could be changed.

That reality led to crippling fear. I was so focused on everything that could go wrong, as Elijah was when he stood on the edge of the pool, that my fear didn't even allow me to think I could jump. I really lived as a victim to the finances within the cycle. It didn't mean I didn't excel in other areas—being a mom and homeschooling—but I allowed the financial cycle to control all the spaces of my life—including opportunity. I believed, during those years, that I was to remain the support, the helpmate, and not say "Enough" and become an active part of the solution.

My cycle?

1. Even though we are poor, my husband will provide and I will take care of the family, but there is the mail carrier with another overdue notice. (reality) ➤

2. If I were worth it (or good enough), then we would have enough money so the results of poverty wouldn't crush me. (agreement) ➤

3. I don't have the ability to change it, and it's not my responsibility, so just be busy. (excuse) ➤

4. And back to a variation of number one. (reality) ➤

In other words, something happens and I make an agreement with myself about my capabilities. Then I find—intentionally or subconsciously—excuses to keep me from making the necessary changes, and thus what I believe becomes and remains a reality.

I *expected* the cycle to spin around, the knocks to happen, and me to stand there and think, *If only I were worthy—or better—this wouldn't happen.* Now instead of periodically watching the road for the kids to return, I'd watch the road like a hawk, nervous if anyone slowed down by our house.

Imagine if you could give physical attributes to a cycle. Picture the diameter of the cycle's initial spin as ten feet. With each cycle's repetition (for example, the knocks), the diameter does not remain at ten feet; it gradually shrinks, allowing the rotation to get faster and more frequent. As the frequency increases, the susceptibility of accepting the cycle as normal also increases.

If you look at my agreement further (*If only I were worthy—or better—this wouldn't happen*), you can see that I did not assign power to myself to change the cycle but made it about intrinsic worth. You cannot make bad events or challenging situations link to self-worth—they are independent.

Yet every door knock strengthened the reality, solidified the agreement, and perpetuated excuses. At one point, as challenging as it was, the cycle felt normal, expected. Rather than thinking I could get out, I reasoned that the cycle was simply the cards I was dealt.

We are not dealt a certain deck of cards in life, and the cards we deal with in our reality are not indicators of worth. For me, the knocks stopped when I valued myself enough to disrupt and stop that cycle's spin. What was the disruption? It was personal responsibility.

I've shared about cycles in many keynote speeches, on my blog, and with my friends. Once we identify cycles, it's easier to become aware of patterns we get stuck in. After telling my friend Darcie what I'd discovered about stuck cycles in life, she was able to begin to identify a cycle she was caught in. Darcie was always chasing happiness but never really achieved it. She would find something that sounded good and initially pursue it with ferocity. But then she would get scared of the responsibility of finishing, and she'd give up.

At one point, she met an Avon lady who was making a lot of extra money. This woman shared how taking the risk of this business venture enabled her to pay for her family to take a trip to Disney World. Darcie loved that idea, had always wanted to take her kids there, and decided she wanted to sell Avon products. She bought all the start-up kits, had a home party, and started with passion. But as the weeks went by, she then realized that to make it profitable, she was going to have to work and put serious effort in and push the boundaries of comfort and practicality. The depth and idea of work didn't come across when she was listening to the Disney World story. So instead of pushing through to the eventual harvest, she gave up.

She told herself that her time would be better spent helping her kids. And then she volunteered to help run the kids' fair at school and said she was just too busy to do Avon well. Does this sound like the excuse of busy? What about the excuse of pride?

But she still was missing something, still had that longing for more, still chased happiness.

Months later she decided she had the skills necessary to be a personal trainer. She spent the money for the course to become certified. She took notes, laminated the pages of notes, took the quizzes, and got all the way to the end, at which point she was required to take a certification exam at one of the approved facilities in town. That meant she'd be mingling with others who were pursuing their personal-training careers. And that also meant she would probably have to work to get clients. All of a sudden, the fear of the unknown spoke louder than the passion of jumping, so she never took the exam.

This time she reasoned with herself that there were too many personal trainers in the area for her to make any money. She told herself she was too busy, the kids too little to have her gone. And then she put all the training materials in the closet. Instead of changing lives, she focused on organizing the Christmas and holiday boxes next to the personal-training courses.

Darcie's cycle?

1. I am unhappy and want some fulfillment. (reality) ➤
2. If I become successful at something, I will have to work hard and might not have time for motherhood, and I'm not that good with people. (agreement) ➤
3. I am too busy—I need to clean my house first. (excuse) ➤
4. I am unhappy and want some fulfillment. (reality) ➤

Her cycle of happiness occurred every year until her almost-finishing-things-but-then-quitting cycle became apparent to her. Does realizing a cycle change it? Absolutely not. But before you can break it, you have to be willing to take an honest assessment of your life to uncover it. What are the events that keep looping? What are the places where you are thinking, *Seriously? Why does this keep happening?* If it feels as though your life is on a continuous-repeat loop, chances are you're repeating a cycle.

The way to break the cycle? It's you irrevocably deciding you have the power to change it.

12

Look Back and Rediscover You

Ending a cycle happens when you put down your pride and decide you want to break free. You can choose to sit in the past and dwell on how many times the cycle has spun, *or* you can decide to use your present moment as the giant wake-up call of life and in that wake-up call set into motion change for your future. Does it matter that you lost years? No. What matters is now.

This present moment is yours. Don't wait for life to slap you in the face with a wake-up call. Don't let excuses slow you down from looking at the cycles you spin in. Even if you think you've been given the worst hand of cards in life, that doesn't mean you can't make something brilliant with them. Use your creativity, the dreamer portion of your childhood, to realize that you don't need to play games with those cards. Instead, you can make an impressive structure. Same cards, different outcome.

This taking control of your life? It is *your* responsibility.

If you want to break whatever unending and hopeless cycle you're in, you have to start with you. I don't mean you become Wonder Woman and add yet another responsibility to your already overflowing mom plate. I don't mean you don't ask for help. I don't mean you become stronger. I mean the change must start with you, in your mind, just as it had to start with me.

Remember my cycle that was seemingly impossible to break? I was wrong. I broke it. I no longer have collectors at my door, my gas bill is fully paid, and my van sits in my driveway without my fearing that it will be repossessed. I know my worth is much greater than I could previously accept. This started with the powerful step of personal responsibility.

There are steps to change—one after another after another.

START WITH YOUR NORMAL

I have this cool friend named Liz. Liz is one of my truth-teller friends. We met online, she knew the speaking and blogging part of me, and as time passed she recognized the masks I still wore regarding my personal life. We were very close in the months leading to my separation. As a result, she could start to see through me and decided not to accept my excuses as acceptable. Rather, she put herself on the line and pushed me to admit the brokenness.

"Describe your normal," she said one summer day. I'm not sure what prompted her to ask, other than my changing the topic quickly when the conversation would get too close to exposing the desperation I lived within. Because of struggling through her own divorce and emotional issues, she was aware of how I might be tempted to hide truth from everyone around me, including those I knew well. "Start at the beginning of a typical day and describe everything that happens."

I started in, talking about my day and the kids and so forth.

It didn't take her long to interrupt me. "Rachel, I want you to know that is not normal."

Her insight surprised and challenged me. I thought I was describing a usual, average, boring day, but she was forcing me to trust that from the outside perspective, what I tolerated on the inside was not rightly ordered. When we hide behind masks for extended periods of time, they have the ability to distort the reality we are living within, and what we deem as normal, or okay, is in fact not.

I was left having to either *accept* her perspective or *deny* her words.

When Liz said that my life wasn't normal, my first instinct was to start excusing away her perspective. My pride wanted to fight and deny the validity of her words, but Liz's truth illuminated the dark hidden spaces in my life. Once they were exposed, once I could see them, I could no longer live unaware. In that moment, I realized that my excuses, the reality I'd accepted as normal, were indeed something I needed to break free from.

No matter how painful, I needed Liz to call me out on my own game. And I needed to accept the calling out. Accepting another person calling you out on your life is a hard spot. Who likes that? Who wants that? But there are moments when we need those who can see clearly to provide clarity to our blurred view of reality.

You need that too. You may not have a friend like Liz, but you have me as your friend—I care about you because I've been in the spot of stuck. We need people in our lives who will say, though it's hard to hear, "Seriously, girl? You think that's right? Why in the world are you afraid? What you are dealing with is not within the continuum of normal. You need to change, and I'm not going to sit back and let you think you don't."

I know how hopeless life can feel at times, how you might feel that it's just going by without purpose, and I want you to break free from the normals you think are destined to remain the same. That's a scary place, those seemingly unchanging realities of cycles. But if you remember the pattern, these cycles can be broken. How? We need to go back to the beginning and remember who we were. We need to rediscover ourselves. And it starts at the agreements.

What happens if you change your agreement? What happens if you decide that because your dreams are important, you will stop excusing "It's not that big a deal" or "It is what it is" moments in life? What happens when you untether yourself from statements that qualify your worth? What happens if you make the agreements about yourself and your potential power? Would you get up twenty minutes earlier to work out if you believed those twenty minutes would not only allow you to have time to yourself but also make you feel better and stronger and happier? Would you get out of that job? Would you turn on a computer and start to write? Would you sign up for that mission trip? Would you go to counseling?

What would you do?

Look at your own normal, your daily timeline. Look at everything you go through every day, the patterns you've adopted, the spaces you excuse away as being "not that big a deal." Then step back and take stock of your entire timeline, not just your everyday normal. As you zoom out, seeing your life from a broader perspective, you will get that first glimpse at some cycles.

What have you accepted as normal that doesn't match the normal of anyone else? Remember that garage-door-scraping-my-back drama I lived with? That was *not* normal. I had to admit I needed help. I also had to admit to myself that I accepted less as normal. In fact, I shared the story with you as an example of something I lived with for years simply dealing with and not fixing. Just because I accepted it does not mean it was right.

Examine your friendships, your relationships, your education, how much stuff you have, your priorities, where you live, what you think you can do, your responsibilities, your dreams—look at it all, everything you accept as your normal and expect to happen in your future. Be aware of all the excuses that will pop into your mind telling you not to spend time there: *Don't do that—it doesn't matter* or *Aren't there dishes to do?*

Fight against those excuses, just as I fought against my pride with Liz, because when we aren't afraid of looking at our patterns, we can diffuse the emotional charge of the timeline. There is no shame in discovering a cycle. This is just an examination. Be clinical, thorough, and if a worry arises, add it to the list. The more logical you are here, the more you will see facts.

So right now, stop and think about your normal.

REEVALUATE YOUR TIMELINE

When I graduated from high school, my mom gathered all the pictures of my youth, arranged them on foam core boards, and presented my story in a line along the back wall of the garage. As my friends and family came to celebrate, they'd walk by the pictures, that unfortunate mullet-hair one included, and comment about not only my journey from babe to adult but also where they fit in and the memories they were part of. It was a collective day of storytelling, of remembering.

My mom had given me a great gift: she'd captured my timeline so I could stand back as the observer and see, well, me. I saw the times I failed, but more than that, I saw the times I excelled. The floral pants, the church moments, the basketball shots. The diplomas, the times at the lake. All of it, in order.

Obviously, my timeline didn't stop that day; it kept going and included my future college years, marriage, kids, bankruptcies, move to Tennessee, speaking career, and writing this book. And despite my not seeing the events beyond today, my timeline extends until a day when I no longer live on this earth. Except on those big moments of graduation, marriage, and impending death, most of us don't step back and examine our timelines. We rarely do that self-inventory, that assessment.

We know analysis is important. Companies chart their year-end; we mark up baby books; we check report cards. Why? Because in the analysis, we discover what worked, what didn't work, and where we need to take a risk. Just like when we unearth cycles and describe normal, our timelines expose our true selves, our dreams, and how and where we need to change or stay firm.

Timelines also establish the length of a cycle's spin and uncover the excuses we give for the cycle.

While writing this book, I took a giant piece of butcher-block paper, rolled it out, and created a physical chart of my timeline. I recorded important things, such as the birth of my kids, but I also listed anything I remembered, good or bad. I shut down the voice that asked me, *Do you really need to include that?* and allowed myself to record seemingly innocent nuances of my story. I wrote down such things as "repo man took the truck" and "spoke at the conference" and "dance recital" and "e-book published" until this timeline was full of hash marks and dates. Then I thought through the why behind each remembered event. Was it really about the repo man? And why that time the repo man came and not the other? What made that significant in my heart? Was it a place of pivot? Did I adopt a new mindset? Did things stay the same or change? What was the emotion? Did I accept responsibility or think, *It is what is,* in that moment?

This is the depth of questions you need to dare ask yourself.

As my sheet became full of marks, the cycle became clear. But I could also see the moments when I attempted to break free of the cycle. Eventually the progress to take control and responsibility shattered the cycle, and a new path won.

When you look at your timeline, can you see a pattern in your own life? Every year when your lease has come up, have you hoped to get a new house but something happened instead? Or have you wanted to get out of that job but tell yourself you will make it one more year? Does something always zap your savings right before your bucket-list trip? Do you have moments when you accept that next year you'll finally get to it?

When you create your timeline and include things like "trip canceled" or "renewed lease" or "annual company picnic," you can begin to identify these cycles. Even though each item is listed as an independent event, there is a deeper structure to each moment. "Trip canceled" means something happened to cancel it. What canceled it? How did it make you feel? Did you plan it again, or did you just let it go?

Now, before you start thinking this is just negative, let me tell you a secret: analysis of your timeline also will bring to light your strengths, tenacity places, and gumption. When I added "started e-book" to my timeline, I demonstrated bravery in the midst of potential hopelessness because right before that was "gas man at the door." The real power comes in figuring out what mindset I adopted that made me dare in that moment and push forward despite dealing with crushing financial realities.

Don't go into this activity thinking you'll be faced by the firing squad of criticism and failure, but rather step back, as I did at my graduation, and assess yourself with a neutral eye. Do not be blind to your own amazing qualities and goodness. Don't minimize yourself, even if life isn't perfect. Here's a truth for you: the fact that you picked up this book and started reading it is a testament to your desire to be brave. That should go on your timeline. Why? Because on that day, you thought, *What could happen if I read this book?*

That's strength. That's faith like Joseph from the Old Testament had. That's thinking you can change your tomorrow. Don't let the hard events fill the timeline—add your triumphs as well.

Remember, your strength might be in a hospital stay or how you dealt with a financial crisis or when you forgave someone you once deemed unforgivable. Your strength might be in the art project you helped your fourth grader believe he could do that earned the blue ribbon. Your strength might be in making dinners with not much food when the budget is tight. It might be in listening to the friend who feels alone.

Your timeline? It should be your normal, your awesome, your struggles, your failures, your successes, and anything else you remember.

Get that piece of paper and start mapping you.

By the way, this is not a five-minute project that will be graded. If you're a grade kind of person, put a 99 percent A on it now so you can move forward. This is a project I hope becomes a posture of living, a new cycle on your timeline. When you are aware of how you exist, you are aware of how you use time, what agreements you make, and what results happen.

This is the timeline of your life. (Cue soap opera music.)

13

Take It One Step, One Inch, at a Time

Let's go back to the "started e-book" hash mark on my timeline. In order to get to the place in life where I would even record that as a significant event means I also had to have events leading up to it. Those events? When I started my blog. That was another tick on my timeline. One led to the other.

At one point in my life, I had to make a decision to blog. That meant, despite all my excuses, I was going to find time within my day to sit down and pursue a passion. When I started, it was just an outlet, somewhere I could share about the ins and outs of homeschooling and motherhood. As time passed, I discovered that this online space gave my heart a voice.

Even though my world was stifling, my writing was freeing.

I didn't start writing thinking it would be the solution to problems. My main goal was, and still is, to be the voice of hope for one other person who feels alone in motherhood. I was finding bravery in removing masks, and the more bravery I discovered, the more I shared with the world.

Needless to say, my blog grew rapidly, which is what led to the "started e-book" hash mark on the timeline. Despite the depth of work putting together and marketing an e-book and my pride whispering fears of *What if no one purchases it?*, I persisted, believing the results would be good. Remember Jim Carrey writing a check to himself (see chapter 8)? I had that outlook.

I didn't sell just a couple of copies—I sold thousands.

Now, truthfully, I could have written the e-book earlier than I did. Yes, part of my own fears and excuses stopped me, but there was one other thing: all the steps from start to completion overwhelmed me and made me procrastinate. The process seemed so daunting that it felt easier to say, *I'll get to that e-book tomorrow,* despite thousands of readers asking for it today. I had to overcome my feelings about the process and the details and embrace that good ol' saying "How do you eat an elephant? One bite at a time."

Details can seem impossible.

Usually we can visualize the result or the goal, but the details, the path to getting there? That's what typically shuts us down. If getting from step one to step ten were easy, then most people would have no issue completing dreams. But this process is not a walk in the park. We generally have excessive stamina for steps one and two, but then step three? If that seems nebulous or scary or too much work, then all of a sudden all the excuses to stop, to wait, to question the path creep in.

If you're an analyzer, as I am, you probably assume that this detail portion would be awesome. But most of the time, I analyze the complexity of how to figure out the details and don't get to actually figuring out the details.

The first thing we need to do is step back from any emotion that makes the details seem impossible to resolve. The less emotion the better. Instead, we are simply going to focus on the order of the steps to make the path from point A to point B easier.

Write It Out

Take out a sheet of paper (I feel like a teacher) and title it "Awesome Dream" or "Awesome Goal" or "What I Need to Change" or whatever cool title you want to give it. Then list what that is.

Here are some examples:

- I need $94,231 to pay old hospital bills.
- I need to leave my abusive boyfriend.
- I want to go back to school and get my degree.
- I want to quit my job and create art full time.
- I want to go to Wednesday-night art class every week.
- I want to train for a marathon.
- I want to volunteer at my kids' school.
- I want to start a book club.

It's critical that you write down what you're trying to accomplish. The clearer you can articulate your goal, the clearer your target will become. When my family and I first moved to Nashville, I made my kids direct us from school to our new home. I told them that despite my being the driver, they were the direction givers. We started at their school, and I turned only where they told me to turn, step by step by step. Not only did it result in laughter, but it also cemented in them the confidence to get home if needed and the ability to navigate the streets. I needed them to know not only where we lived but also how to get there from the starting place of school. I wanted them to see the details.

It's the same for you and me: we need to be clear on our goals and express them with confidence.

Brainstorm, and then under your stated goal, list every single task you need to do to make it happen. (By the way, keep out your worry list. You'll hear worries. Remember, they are excuses. Just write them down and then move on.) To create change, you need to pause and ask yourself,

What steps do I think I need to take?, and consider any and all that come to mind. (You do not need to list the steps in order.)

Bear in mind, this is a brainstorm. This is not the place or time to debate what you come up with. If you're going to work on cleaning out the garage and you decide one of the items on your list should include putting all the boxes outside the garage so you can see and organize them better, write that down. Don't let a thought like *But what will the neighbors think?* stop you from listing all the details you come up with.

For my move to Nashville, I listed all sorts of things: find the school, register the kids at school, find a doctor, get packing boxes, find a moving truck, clean out under the deck, sort the garage, transfer records, find a new house, talk to my parents, register for schools, get rid of the junk. And mixed in all of that, I included the normal mom stuff of birthdays and homework and needing to take a breath and working and having moments of freak-out because I was moving.

All that made it onto my list.

Nothing is too small or insignificant to include on your list. Again, do not question or overanalyze or edit what you put down. Just brainstorm. There are no wrong answers, no thoughts without merit. The point is to unearth worries, problems, and potentials that will affect your accomplishing your goal.

Here's another example we talked about earlier: a Wednesday-night art class. Suppose life would be glorious if you could just meet your friends for art every Wednesday night at seven. You went once before and enjoyed it, but life's busyness has had a way of preventing you from attending regularly. You know that you are excusing yourself, yet the details of how to make it work just seem too crazy. However, because you value yourself and want to fuel your passions, you decide that somehow you're going to start going every week. Write that goal at the top of your paper: "Art Class on Wednesday Night."

Now you need to look at the details of how to make it happen. In order to go to art class every Wednesday, you start to list:

- I need my family's support.
- The kids should have their homework done.
- I'll need money to buy the supplies.
- Dinner should be thought out and prepared.
- Trash must be collected and put outside for early trash pickup.
- My car should be fueled up.
- I won't allow guilt to hold me back.

And so forth . . .

That's a brainstorm.

What are the things in your world that would need to be done to make your goal a reality? Write them all down. Then look over the list again. Do you have to personally make sure all these things are completed? For instance, if your spouse is on board, perhaps he can handle dinner, trash collecting, and homework-checking details. As you go back over the list, you may find you can get rid of some steps and need to add others, but as a whole this is your action list.

Then you have to be able to say with 100 percent certainty, *If all this is true, I can make Wednesday art class a regular thing.* If you deem this as important as the harvest, everything else to be done can be handled in a different way because the corn needs to be picked.

This is important. *This is you*—your heart, your talents, your refueling.

Many times you will come to a place where everything will be in order and you still won't budge. That is self-sabotage, and it will stop you from attempting something new. This list is often where you look for excuses from the previous section. Trust me, they'll be screaming at times.

As you look at your list (which will probably be quite long), ask yourself which detail or step or task is making you tell yourself that this change or goal is impossible. There are always solutions. They might not be the easiest, most glamorous, most enjoyable solutions, but there are still solutions. You have to open your mind to them. Stay in search mode and write down any overwhelming details without allowing this process to make your heart race.

The impossible detail is the only important one. The rest are simply steps. Remember how to eat the elephant? The steps are the bites.

ORDER YOUR LIST

Now take another piece of paper and see if you can put your list in chronological order, which is one *very* important step. You need to figure out which tasks are dependent on others. This is so critical, especially if you're a worrier. You don't want to worry about tasks you're not ready to tackle. Too many times we ponder step seven before we've even begun. But until we get to step four, we might not even know what step seven will completely look like, and all we accomplish in its place is wasting time.

For instance, at this point, worrying that you don't have the right materials for art class is fruitless. You have a lot of things to figure out before you're even sure you can go. Worry about the supplies after you've paid the tuition.

Let's go back to the art-class example and break it down further. Look at the item "Dinner should be thought out and prepared," and break that into parts. What would need to happen to ensure that dinner would be ready? You'd have to train the kids to make it themselves? You'd have to turn Wednesday into a leftovers day? You'd pick something up? Or you'd have to do it yourself but in a different way? Could you get up earlier on Wednesdays so you could start the slow cooker and still make it to the ridiculously long car line in time to pick up your kids from school? To get to art night, you would need to solve this dinner issue.

If you decide to make Wednesday a slow-cooker day, you'll need to add the required items to your weekly shopping list so you can prep in the morning. You also will want to remember on Tuesday night to set the alarm for an earlier time so you can ensure that "I didn't get dinner ready" isn't a reason not to make it to art class. All those excuses for not doing Wednesday-night art class (or coffee night or whatever) are all places that you agreed not to move or change. When you make that list, you debunk the excuses, all of them, and create a climate of change.

Although this may seem to be a small example of a goal, the point is the same: your job is to figure out the path for making what you need or want to do go from "not happening" to a "possibility" to a new "reality."

Then write down the next item on your list. Determine what needs to happen to make it possible, and plan for it. A dream without a plan is a dream. A dream with a plan is a reality.

When you put all the tasks in chronological and logical order, you create steps to make your goal come to fruition. I know it might feel silly to list all these details, but let me ask you this: How many times do you think about all these things and let that thinking and wondering and worrying preoccupy your mind?

And if you've ever used the excuse "I can't make it because I didn't plan dinner for the kids," you have fallen prey to an unresolved detail-derailing process. The fact that you can list details like this means you've been thinking them but have never listed them.

This kind of list and attention to the details works for every single space where you need to make change, and it helps equip you for navigating the speed bumps so they don't detour or derail you. What's a speed bump? It is something that makes people stop and think that something is not working. It is a stopping place. You need to see the speed bumps—quite often the details—as things to solve, to push through, that once fixed will propel you toward your goal. They are the situations in which you should push on, push forward, push through.

Now stop and breathe.

All you are going to do is create your list. That's it. You are not traveling to the moon. You are not writing a documentary. You are not trying to solve climate change. You are just writing all the things you think you need to do to start moving toward the goal.

Once you brainstorm and look over that giant list, you're going to find the first thing to solve. You'll uncover things you're worrying about that don't deserve your time and give clarity to a path of progress.

Do you remember the end date you chose for your goal back in chapter 7? This is why it is critical. These steps to change need an end date, a day that will come no matter what, when you can step back and assess your journey. Without the specific date, you can use all the excuses in the world to never get to what you need to do, pushing it off until tomorrow. Ponder this. In the sixties, President Kennedy didn't just tell the world that one day America would potentially go to the moon. Instead, he very clearly stated we would land on the moon before the end of the decade. That date? That became the target, and there was no doubt that every single step, every failure, every success would lead to completion. On July 20, 1969, two Americans were the first humans to land on the moon, completing the goal. It is just as critical that your date has as much weight as going to the moon, because without that specificity, it just becomes something that you could get to someday.

With your date in mind, look through what you wrote on your list and determine which item is step one. Write a one by it. Then find steps two, three, four, and so on. You'll find that some steps are dependent on previous ones, and once you start moving, you will create a chain reaction of movement.

The inertia will have shifted from potential energy to kinetic energy. Once change happens, it doesn't just meander—it explodes.

TACKLING EMOTIONS

Occasionally, making this list and attacking these decisions gets clouded by emotions. I've alluded to that in the emotional-bond excuse section, but let's dissect it further with some excuse-buster tactics designed to keep you from deterring momentum.

My move to Nashville, which resulted in all the planning and purging we've discussed, happened about eighteen months ago. People always wonder why I moved so far, and truthfully, beyond the business opportunity and my parents needing to sell the house we lived in, there was a great deal of emotional baggage left in my Minnesota home. Nashville was a fresh start, a clean slate, and unlike when we moved to San Diego, I wasn't moving to hide but rather to be free to invest in a future timeline with opportunity.

Did that make it easy? No. Through almost every step of my cross-country move, my emotions were running high. I was relocating my kids from the only home most of them knew. I was moving us far from family. We all experienced anxiety, nervousness, fear, sadness, and excitement swirling together and quite often clouding the finite nature of each step.

To put my plan into action, I needed to strip the emotion from the goal.

You'll need to do that too.

There will be many days when your internal soundtrack will sound like this: *How in the world am I going to get this all done? I'm crazy! What was I thinking?*

That's how it was for me. With each step, I had to navigate the emotions afresh.

I've been there, been a slave to emotion, so I understand this well. It took me four years to create a new normal for my family after my divorce. What we're discussing in these pages took me eight years to figure out and implement. It's been eleven years since I first met my counselor, Ed. It's been thirty years since those boys called me ugly. I'm not expecting you to break new frontiers tomorrow, as if you'll easily be able to wish changes into existence overnight. Don't set yourself up for failure by thinking this is as effortless as painting a wall or planting a flower or even boiling water. This stuff is emotionally, suck-the-life-out-of-you hard. Since I want to be the voice of truth, I will not minimize the effort. All those sessions with Ed left me motivated but tired.

But just because something is difficult doesn't mean we should stop.

Our timeline doesn't stop for the hard moments. Life doesn't slow down when you have your ducks in a row. You might not feel ready for many of these steps, and there is nothing wrong with that. You cannot boil water until the pot is actually on the stove. Reading this book might be the first time you've dared to think, *Do I even own a pot?* In other words, this might be the first time you see your life and actually attempt to find joy and happiness again.

When I say you might not feel ready, it's because of that "stick to it, fall seven times, stand up eight times" kind of work that's the inevitable part of change. But whether you feel you're prepared or not, you can accomplish almost everything—hard, life-changing work included. It doesn't matter what it is. Getting a new job, losing two hundred pounds, paying off $100,000 in debt, raising a child—you can accomplish any and all of them, even if the problem seems totally out of your control or far from practicality.

It's in the details—tackling them one at a time.

Every inch you tackle is an inch closer. Those inches don't remain inches. Twelve of them and you have a foot of change. Twenty-four more and you have a yard. Pretty soon that small inch is a mile. But you don't get to a mile until you decide that you are worth fighting for the first inch.

Today marks your first day of claiming your inches of change.

Let the fight begin.

14

Choose the Right Mental Targets

I find reasons to go to Target. I credit this wonderful excuse to my mom and all my trips there in my youth. And despite the "Hey, ugly" incident, Target is like my own almost-free therapy. I can enter crabby and exit happier—even if I buy nothing, which rarely happens and is why this therapy isn't really free. My kids joke that our van has its crosshairs on Target, because we'll always make a stop there for something.

The mental words we tell ourselves are powerful targets too. Picture an actual target in your mind, the concentric circles, and imagine that the bull's-eye center has a word written on it. If you were shooting arrows and the bull's-eye said "100," you'd get a hundred points for hitting it. The goal is to aim for the center so you get the results/reward of hitting that spot. Just as I can find reasons to wander at Target, our brains find reasons, supporting actions, to hit the targets in our minds that we have set. So we need to set the ones that will move us forward, not hold us back.

THE BULL'S-EYE

The mental targets we set can be either positive or negative, leading toward or away from a desired outcome. But beyond that, the words we say can actually create an intended or unintended target for our goals. For example, think about this phrase: "Hurry up—we are going to be late."

I'm not sure about you, but that seems to be a quote from my almost-everyday morning routine with my kids. It's a race against the clock, dealing with grade schoolers who are dawdling and not eager to get in the van for school. It might seem that I tell them this because I don't want them marked tardy, which I clearly do not, but underneath that ring of thought is this deeper truth: I hate being late.

Some of my kids, as we've already established, do not share my love of punctuality. If I tell them it's time to leave, for them it inevitably means it's now time to go to the bathroom, find socks, get something to drink, look for the backpack that used to be by the door, get another drink, now look for the shoe that also used to be by the door, and finally meander down the stairs to the open door with me waiting impatiently. Nothing gets under my skin more than seeing dillydallying when the late-for-school clock is ticking. When I say, "Let's go now," I want to *leave* in that very second; however, they think we are merely starting the process to leave.

A communication issue and a habit issue, right? You want to tell me to make the time to leave earlier? To change the clock ahead five minutes and not let them know? To place the shoes by the door?

What if instead of tricks and new plans, we reverse the culture and the entire process by altering what we say? Go with me here because this will change your perspective.

If I tell my kids, *"Hurry up! We are going to be late!"* then I have established a target.

The target is this: we are going to be *late*. And everyone needs to hurry so we can be late.

Late is the bull's-eye, the word in the "100" spot.

If we aim for late, we're going to be late, because everyone hears, "We are going to be late," and their actions bring about what we verbalized—and we hit this unintended target.

What happens if the target is switched?

My goal for the family was always to get them to school before the bell rang. Whether I used *late* or *early,* we were still going to accomplish the bigger goal of arriving at school. It is important to note that even with negatively framed targets, we typically have a positive goal and intention. No one intentionally aims for late. Can you think of a situation in which you would yell, "Hey, guys, slow down with what you're doing because I want to be late"? Yet despite our not seeking to be late, we still use the word *late* as the ultimate target.

So how do we switch it? We replace the language of the target. Instead of my running around like the frantic mom reminding everyone how all the hurrying is going to lead to our lateness, what if I change it to "Let's get going so we are early"?

I just created a new target: *early.*

Whether we are aware of it or not, a simple switch in vocabulary changes where everyone shoots the arrows. And where we point our arrows is a powerful indicator of future success.

Late versus early. Scarcity versus abundance. Bitterness versus joy. Worrying versus planning.

What if we reframed the messages we communicate to our brains?

Look at these before-and-after examples:

GOAL: Clean house

Target 1: The house is such a mess that I don't even know where to start cleaning.

Target Reframed: Start in one room, go to the next, and soon the house will be clean.

Target Comparison: *mess* versus *clean*

GOAL: Respectful kids

Target 1: Stop sassing back to me. You are so disrespectful.

Target Reframed: You are to talk respectfully to me. You have integrity.

Target Comparison: *disrespectful* versus *have integrity*

GOAL: Speaking in front of the women's group

Target 1: Don't stumble over your words.

Target Reframed: Breathe deeply, slow down, and speak confidently.

Target Comparison: *stumble* versus *speak confidently*

GOAL: Homework finished

Target 1: Why are you making this so hard?

Target Reframed: I get that this is challenging, but you will figure it out.

Target Comparison: *hard* versus *figure it out*

When you rethink your target, you gain control over your life. You can reframe your targets and teach your kids to do the same. In fact, my family and I have used this method so much now that my kids will call me out on the times I forget and urgently yell that we're going to be late. One frantic Monday morning as we rushed to get in the van for school, I forgot my words and said, "We're going to be late." Samuel, who was in second grade at the time, replied, "Great, now we really *will* be late."

That is the power of changing the words, the targets, for your goals.

REFRAME YOUR MESSAGES

Reframing your mental messages takes time and practice and work—many times hard, persistent work. It also means you continue to listen to your internal dialogue. You can't catch that you're telling yourself that you're going to be late until you hear yourself speaking it as truth.

It's virtually impossible to move forward without doing this mental work. You could read this chapter and move on to the next without giving the material another thought. Or you could decide to dig deep and apply it to your life even if it feels strange. If you've never listened to your thoughts, this is a new concept. But there is a reason we are to renew our minds. It's so we hear truth and can expose targets that seem right but actually are cutting ourselves short. I like to think of it as fast food versus real food, really. Which do you want? Which is better for you in the long run?

All the target statements you work to transform will become powerful trajectories for your life goals. Humor me. Close your eyes—but not for too long because I need you to read—pause for a couple of minutes, breathe deeply, and listen. I want you to hear everything: the hum of the furnace, the dishwasher running, the mail carrier driving by. But more than that, I especially want you to listen to your thoughts. What pops into your mind? Is it a reminder telling you to do something? Is it an overwhelming feeling, such as anxiety? Is it a calm whispering of good things? Is it a voice asking, *What on earth are you doing right now listening to your thoughts?*

Take two minutes and just try it. Tune in to yourself.

True introspection allows us to see, hear, and feel what is and challenge our own status quo. I learned that part of my thinking was negative. Imagine if all your thoughts and emotions could gather in one space, such as a boardroom. You're in charge, but there they are: fear, boredom, the part of you that worries about appearance, the part of you that giggles over silly movies, the part of you that frets over finances, the part of you that loves long walks. Once you're looking at all the parts that make you whole, you might see one part: pessimism. Well, I'm telling you,

I have that pessimistic part. I refer to that part of my thinking as Ms. GlassEmpty. For a long time, until I decided not to let that aspect of my thinking have so much power, Ms. GlassEmpty thought her pessimistic side was in charge of hope, optimism, and planning.

Just to set the record straight here, this is merely a thought pattern. I've characterized it only as a "part" to add clarity to the power of target statements.

For years, the thought pattern of Ms. GlassEmpty tainted my belief in the future. The deep fear was that I would always be poor. If my bull's-eye was "poor," I relied on the excuse of scarcity to keep that "poor" target in the bull's-eye.

For the cycle to break and new results to happen, I had to take captive the pessimistic part of my thinking and lead it to optimism. I didn't intentionally adopt pessimism as a target, just as most of us don't decide that this year will be full of trouble. However, after years of not only staying stuck but also getting deeper in debt and hoping for a financial breakthrough, the pessimistic part developed as a way to protect me from getting hurt. If I was pessimistic about an opportunity, I wouldn't get hurt when that opportunity fell apart. Sounds great, right? Except, when you really think about it, just like when I had aimed for late, I was aiming for poor.

As an alternative to getting angry and frustrated at myself and my previous tendency toward pessimism, I needed to refute the pessimistic thought cycle and replace it with truth. The truth is that I aim for abundance, not poverty. The truth is that I want to see the possibility, not what could go wrong. Instead of immediately debating situations, I've developed an optimistic yet calculated risk-taking part of my thought process.

You can do this too. But you have to be aware of the inner dialogue and projected outcomes that you accept as unchangeable.

We need to be in charge of not just *what* we think but *how* we think.

STOP FIGHTING OPTIMISM

Most nights I ask my kids to tell me three things from their day that made them happy. They can be simple, small moments—such as shoelaces staying tied for gym or getting an extra scoop of double chocolate chip ice cream—or they can be bigger things, such as that birthday party invitation they received or counting down the days until school break and feeling the excitement of vacation getting closer and closer. Right now my Samuel will tell you that there are nine weeks left until summer break, that he loves the Lego videos on YouTube, and that orange Tic Tacs are his favorite. The exercise isn't to look for massive rewards but rather to train the brain to seek out the positive, the optimistic moments—the good. It also helps my kids see that their efforts toward an end goal—the trying hard, digging deep, taking the extra step—deserve accolades just as much as the completion of that goal. We've learned to celebrate the inches in the process. If they tell me they're excited about getting an 80 percent on multiplication facts instead of seeing that they got 20 percent wrong, we celebrate the good and vow to get a better grade next time. This is disciplined gratitude—being happy and thankful and allowing that joy to encourage the inch of now as well as motivate progression to a higher goal.

This type of thinking is intentionally seeking what worked versus what didn't work. It's having the confidence to say, *Wow, today I'm really proud I pushed through that job,* rather than focusing on how frustrating that job was.

When you start to make moves, claiming those inches, disrupting your normal, you will change your trajectory, your target, and with that boost in confidence comes ripples. That is why it's critical to practice pinpointing what you've accomplished, so the negative, pessimistic, doubting part of yourself gets extinguished by the bravery of confidence.

Motherhood's intensity can magnify what isn't working. We see the

towels left on the bathroom floor versus the clean kids. We see the unfin-
ished homework versus the child who tried. We see the empty pantry and
wrappers left on the counter versus the food we provided. We see markers
on the walls versus a home we live in. We see how we got frustrated with
our children for not remembering multiplication facts versus the time we
spent side by side studying.

We can easily see the negative and miss the good. We just have to re-
train our brains to focus on particular parts of our lives. When I have my
kids share with me awesome things that happened during their days, we
are, as a family, exercising our minds to seek out the positive. It also forces
me—the one who can slip into a state of overwhelm, excuses, and pessimism—to back out of thinking, *Woe is me. I am a bad mom because the
van was ridiculously messy when I dropped off my second grader in the
school line and everyone saw the mess, including the fast-food wrappers,
and now they will think not only that I can't handle stuff but also that
we eat terribly,* and into thinking, *Way to go. It was a crazy morning, the
kids were exhausted, you lost the lunch box, you thought you were going
to be late, but you got them there in the school line and managed to yell,
'Have a great day,' while the van door closed.*

It's all perspective and how you empower yourself with your own
descriptors.

These thoughts amplify progress: when we look for joy, for optimism, the door always opens for more joy, more optimism. Once we
learn to refocus our pessimism, we unleash great power. That power? The
life-changing power of "what if."

WHAT IF

I never thought I could be a runner. More than that, I would boldly inform
everyone there was *no way* that they would ever witness me running.

I convinced myself that I was capable only of team sports. Honestly, I believed I would be the worst runner in the world because I couldn't motivate myself to keep running when my legs got tired or my breathing labored. If you're not a runner, you need to know that most runners fight leg or breath fatigue. My excuse for not running was that, for most of my life, when I'd hit places of fatigue, I couldn't figure out how to push myself and not stop. As soon as my breathing became heavy, it was a valid reason for me to quit running.

In my neighborhood in Nashville, a fantastic trail follows the road between my home and the elementary school. Every morning as I waited in line to drop off my little boys at school, I'd glance over and watch the runners plodding by on that paved path. After a couple of weeks, I started recognizing the runners: the wild-legging lady, the man who struggles to keep up with his female partner, the older man with the white fluffy dog.

And then one day to my surprise, I thought, *What if I ran?*

At first all my old excuses, my limiting factors, my pessimistic self shut down my "what if" hoping. I had no time, didn't have good shoes, needed some cool running pants, and so forth. For several weeks I treaded in the "what if" spot, until one day I listened to the "what if" more than the excuses. That day, after returning home from school, I went upstairs, threw on some running capris and a T-shirt, laced up my black Adidas running shoes that I'd never run in, walked back down the stairs, opened the door, and started to run.

I should have started by walking, but I didn't know. So that first day, I ran.

Confession: I was the worst.

My pride was screaming at me to stop, to not let others see me at this beginning place. But my legs didn't listen to my brain, and just as Elijah had jumped into the pool, I ran.

I didn't know about pacing and split times. I really couldn't breathe.

I tried to hide that I was hyperventilating. When a car passed, I'd attempt to close my mouth, which was open because I was panting so badly. My lungs felt as though an elephant were sitting on them and my legs as if I wore weighted leggings. Even though I pushed through ego, I still didn't want those random drivers to confirm, even if it was just in passing, my rookie running skill. So there I would be, out of breath, pretending to run, even though it was a jog, trying to look as if I had it all together, despite feeling as though I was going to fall over.

Sometimes when you make a change, you have to pretend—not in the mask way, where you never move forward and you pretend stagnation is okay, but in the way where you know you have no clue what you are doing, but you still put on the game face and give it all you've got. Ever heard "Fake it till you make it"? It's that kind of belief. No one is saying, "Fake it till you pretend to make it." The target is *you will make it.* Every day that you practice that belief in your future becomes a day when the pretending to know what you're doing shifts to actually learning, getting better, and achieving what you're working on.

Here's what you need to know about my running: I always made it back home. Despite wanting to stop. Despite having no breath in my lungs. Despite starting a love-hate relationship with Advil.

I kept lacing up those shoes and walking out the door and running down the street.

As the days passed, I began to understand the hills. I knew I had to shorten my stride so I could make it up a hill without my legs giving out. I established goals—make it to the crosswalk or to the park—and I set time limits. I no longer cared what the people in the cars thought about me; I now cared about running. I'd push myself to run just a bit farther, another couple of feet, and gradually those feet and blocks added up to miles. Then one day my running app congratulated me on running two hundred miles. For the girl who never thought she would run, that acknowledgment proved one thing: I was stronger than the beliefs I assumed were unchangeable.

All because I opened myself to a possibility that I never considered was one.

Look back at your dream-goal list. Is there a "what if" item missing from it? Is there that one thing you want to try but your pride is holding you back? Is there this crazy thing you want to do—skydive, paint with wax, get a tattoo, sing karaoke (which I find terrifying)—but you have refrained? It is vital that your "what if" places are added to your list.

Everyone I have ever known who has skydived is proud of having done so.

Everyone who finishes an Ironman triathlon is proud as well.

At one point they, too, had to ask, *What if I skydived or did the Ironman?* It doesn't just happen.

It's action.

What if your "what if" is exactly what your heart needs?

COURSE CORRECTORS

There were times when I didn't have the clarity of the moment to reframe my mental message and target statements. Life preoccupies us with busy, and when there are challenges, the last thing most of us want to be told is "Slow down, breathe, regain perspective, alter your target," because these are moments of pushing through and of doubt. They are also the moments when the normal chaos of life likes to tip the scales to overwhelming moments. In order to keep positive momentum as well as fight fear, it's imperative we create an easy, go-to way to keep ourselves on track. Think of it as the built-in course correction for your mind. Many new vehicles have a supersophisticated driving system that can detect if you're veering over the center line, and if so, the vehicle will course-correct the automobile independent of the driver. If you're the driver, you will feel the correction as a vibration in the steering wheel.

The reason? Sometimes even the most diligent drivers can get off track or distracted, and this course-correcting defense keeps not only the driver and passengers safe but others too.

We get off track as well. If I'm not careful, I can spiral into a pit of worry and anxiety, and before you know it, the simplest of things, such as a late homework assignment, can have me thinking I'm the worst mom in the world, my kids will be failures forever, and I should be relieved of my title of Mom. Because I know I have this tendency, I've built course-correcting parameters into my life.

One of my solutions is to listen to music.

When I run, I always have my earbuds in and Pandora on. I listen to loud music with a steady beat, music about victory and pushing through no matter what. The music becomes the cheerleader, drowning out my own thoughts of *I can't do this* or *I am tired* or *My legs hurt* and replacing them with courage and confidence. The words and rhythm distract me from my own doubts and keep me in the lane of running.

In the months after my separation, when I wasn't sure what to do next because the list of stuff to finish was huge and my soundtrack of doubts deafening, I listened to OneRepublic's "Marchin On" for hours on end. The lyrics repeat over and over the idea of moving forward, of putting "one foot right in front of the other."[9] To me, it was about moving forward and, to use their words, "marchin on" as a course-correcting safeguard. Instead of listening to *I don't know what to do,* I replaced it with *I'm marching on.* That target correction bolstered my confidence and replaced heels-in-the-ground fear with action.

Music may not have the same outcome for you, but don't let that stop you from rewriting your internal soundtrack with positive targets and course-correcting defenses to keep you moving toward your goals.

If you struggle with feeling as though you are not enough, get out a big permanent marker and write "I am enough" on sticky notes and put them all over your house so you don't veer sideways. If you get agitated before going to work, add a meditation app to help you be still for fifteen minutes beforehand. Have a go-to friend who will help replace your worrisome thoughts with empowering statements. Change your phone's home screen so that it displays a message reminding you to breathe deeply. My home screen says, "Fear loses grip on a brave soul." Why? Because I identify myself as brave, and thus fear has no grip on my decisions or qualification of self.

Sometimes staying on course can occur by changing your environment. Go run, go to the gym, go to Starbucks, go to a friend's house, go to the living room to get away from the mess in the kitchen, do what you need to do. But break the negative pull that slows down progress.

Music, location, notes, verses of truth, friends—these are all resources to help you renew and gain control of your mind. It's time for course correction. You know the goal, and you know where you veer off.

Change the targets and build in the course corrections, and your success, speed, and outlook will improve.

ANCHOR YOUR MINDSET

On my left wrist I wear a black rip-cord bracelet. It is nothing fancy, nothing pretty, but I do not take it off unless required to, such as when going in for surgery. This bracelet is an anchor point in my life.

I purchased this bracelet for three dollars from a local vendor on my first trip to Haiti. That was several months prior to my separation and was during that already established intense period in my life. Beyond the finances, I was also battling my own inner demons—my agreements about marriage and my own heartache at the struggles of a marriage dissolving. Fear was crippling.

It was in the rolling green mountains of Haiti that I confronted my relationship with God from the *Why me? Don't I matter?* days of standing in my snow-covered driveway to *I have the bravery to do hard things.* Moving from being a victim to taking responsibility is a necessary shift. Doing so was when I realized just how much I'd allowed all the stuff that had happened to me to act as a weight to deaden my potential, and as the days passed, as I met people with undeniable bravery, I began to unleash this bravery within myself.

It was imperative to me to bring home an item from Haiti, one that reminded me of the perspective I'd gained there. I didn't want to slip back to the *Why me?* target but knew, from my history, it was an easy mindset to fall into, especially unchecked, without a course correction. For a couple of days, I looked around, yet nothing spoke to me as the right choice. However, on the last night of my time there, some of the locals of the village brought their handmade goods to the outside of our hotel. I knew it was now or never that I find my item.

I walked up and down, searching for my bravery reminder. I don't know what made me think that this simple plastic-covered wire bracelet was the answer, but it's what I chose. After I handed my money over, I took the gray-and-black bracelet, put it on, and have kept it there since. It's now withstood years and years on my wrist. And when my perspective is challenged, when I venture close to slipping into an old pattern, that basic bracelet made by a Haitian woman serves as my anchor.

Yes, anchor. It is an anchor because in Haiti I made a conscious and powerful decision *never* to return to the mindset of victim. I was no longer going to allow others or circumstances to limit my ethos or potential.

Anchors are the strongest, most powerful mindset moments in our lives. An anchor is a place where we decide, *I will* never *go back to that old cycle of thinking.*

Never. The universal qualifier. Anchors are the places in life where we always use it.

An anchor moment happened in my mind that week in Haiti. Think of an anchor as a line in the sand, where once you draw it you will not go back. I was never going to be a victim again. Deciding not to live as a victim created a new bravery—I moved and made decisions and took charge without knowing all the steps or having all the resources. My target wasn't survival, wasn't "it is what it is" but was instead a ferocious determination to live my days with intentionality and vivacious exuberance. I wanted to live with courage, carrying my head high, valuing my life and the life of my children more than staying stuck waiting for life to change.

Even though we make anchor decisions in our brains, oftentimes we need an outer representation of the inner anchor to remind us we are never going back. I have friends who have tattoos on their wrists that remind them of who they are striving to be. For me, at least now, my simple bracelet is the physical reminder of a pivotal mental anchor point in life.

When you break a cycle, you *must* create that mental anchor.

You must decide you're not slipping back.

Having a physical representation of the anchor moment is the most powerful course-correcting, target-driving thing you can do. Do you know why? Your anchor decision isn't rooted in the old cycle but is an upward and forward movement, cementing the new agreement in your life.

Find that anchor, whether it's a tattoo, a photo, or a three-dollar bracelet. Let it remind you that you are not who you were. Set your mind.

15

It's Okay to Freak Out

When I was young, I was fascinated by stories of the pioneers. I loved anything to do with the settlers of the West and read every book I could find about them, adored the *Little House on the Prairie* television show and the books, and played *The Oregon Trail* on a now-vintage computer. The stories of the pioneers' bravery, of heading west in search of freedom and opportunity, inspired me, the schoolgirl trying to fit in, to look beyond the small and dream of the big. I'm still in awe of these trailblazers, still astounded by their courage, but I now have the curiosity of an adult about their experiences. When did they wrestle with wondering if they'd made a mistake? How far along the trail, how many miles from the Independence, Missouri, starting point did that happen? At what time did they have that moment of panic, that freak-out, that point where they were too far from where they'd left and yet still had so far to go?

They couldn't turn back and they couldn't stop moving forward.

I'm sure they experienced anxiousness, doubt, fear, anger, regret, exhilaration, and panic as they dealt with the effects of the trail. It had to have been a swirling mess of contradictions, not just physically but emotionally. But they couldn't stop moving west. They had to deal with not only their own internal worries but also the realities of the risky decision they'd made: surviving the winter, the conflict, the hunger, the harshness of the journey.

But they had made a decision. It wasn't halfhearted, and there was no turning back.

More than four hundred thousand people made the choice to leave the safety of their present and travel west in hopes of tomorrow's future.[10] And because of that drive, that vision, they woke up, day after day, and marched on.

They were in great transition, or as I like to call it, the freak-out. I prefer *freak-out* because it captures the emotion. Transition seems timid, while freak-out, well, it's crying-in-sobs, shaking-in-your-boots intense. The freak-out is the moment when you cannot turn back. Life cannot revert to the past.

Oregon Trail moments in life happen two ways: either we make a decision to never turn back or life forces us on a new path. It does not matter which way starts the change, but that pivot, that moment when we embark into new territories, has within it that freak-out depth.

Don't be ashamed of the freak-out. Don't be embarrassed. Don't run from it either. Be reassured that if you get to the point of the freak-out, it means you're taking action.

When You Can't See the Horizon

My youngest son, Samuel, was diagnosed with celiac disease when he was sixteen months old. Life with celiac disease means that everything you once called normal no longer exists. This setback in life wasn't optional— this was a "life-and-death, adapt, and deal with the results" situation that so many of us get dealt. Prior to his diagnosis, Samuel was fading away, and while it was a relief to be able to fight the disease, the reality of life taking an unexpected path caused a freak-out period.

I didn't realize how much of a gift not thinking about gluten was until the day I could no longer walk into any restaurant and freely order and when the ease of grocery shopping shifted to a slow, painstaking task. I could no longer push my cart down the aisle and grab flour to make cookies. And when Samuel was diagnosed in early 2011, the world wasn't as aware of gluten free. That meant that in most grocery stores, there was barely anything that was safe for him to eat. It also meant that everything he could eat was also, due to the lower supply, exceptionally expensive.

It was a freak-out space.

Grocery shopping used to be an escape, but with the words "Your son can *never* eat gluten," it became a trail I didn't want or know how to traverse. Now beyond having to keep a running tally of the cost of groceries, I was also forced to examine the labels of every single item that entered my cart. There weren't any apps then. I would bring thick gluten-free guides to the store and thumb through the pages, trying to identify safe foods. There were other times when I'd be on the phone with food manufacturers, verifying if the listed modified food starch was gluten free. At first you might think "no bread" is not hard to manage. But "no bread" is for people cutting carbs. Gluten free involves way more than not eating bread. For those with celiac disease, it means you absolutely must not ingest gluten, a protein found in wheat, barley, and rye; if you do, it triggers an autoimmune response that destroys the intestinal lining. When the lining is destroyed, it means you are no longer able to absorb nutrients, which means you starve, despite eating. The only cure?

Never ever eat gluten.

But the transition to gluten free is a monumental learning curve, especially if you've lived your entire life one way. The day Sam went gluten free was the day I, because I am his mom and needed to understand how to live this way, went gluten free. It was rough. I craved bread, noodles, licorice. My word, the cracker aisle would break me, especially the

Goldfish crackers. I'd see them, a favorite for all my kids, and walk by with frustration, when previously I would have grabbed two bags without thinking twice about the ingredients. My tears were angry tears. They were overwhelmed tears. I felt robbed of a life that I was now forced to change. Then I felt guilty because shouldn't I at least have been grateful it wasn't worse? It was this messy dichotomy of grief and guilt that culminated in tears by the crackers.

But because I loved my son and knew that his life was in the balance, I never gave up. I used that *Braveheart* strength. I pushed us forward, walked down this new trail, converted our family's diet to almost 100 percent gluten free (my other kids still eat an occasional frozen pizza or regular bread slice), and became the voice of possibility, focusing on what we could have, not on what we'd lost.

Don't let anyone dismiss the freak-out moments of change. They are challenging and often scary. And when you make such a life pivot, when you are in the midst of other pressures, even simple incidents can be the last straw. There were more times than I can count when I would stand in the grocery store with tears in my eyes as I watched everyone around me pushing carts with items I was no longer allowed to buy.

Wait, I was allowed to buy those items. I could have put them in the cart. But when Sam's biopsy came back positive for celiac disease, I made a choice to accept that reading. And that was the first day of our journey west.

Freaking out doesn't mean you aren't on the right path.

I can imagine the pioneers sitting around the campfire at night and chatting about all the rivers, paths, towns, and impossibilities they'd had to push through. I'm sure they reflected on those who didn't survive, on the times when they thought the wagon wouldn't make it up the hill, and on the horrible sicknesses endured as well as all the places of laughter and the anticipation of what was coming. But they also, especially those early settlers, didn't fully anticipate the arduous length of time on the trail or the setbacks or the feeling of being lost. The moments of "Can you believe we forded the river instead of taking a ferry?" and "We probably should have waited a couple more days for the snow to melt" weren't as clear in the *middle* of the journey. Only once the pioneers had passed through those hardships could they see how the transition could have been faster because there was a quicker route. Only in the end could they see the different trails they followed that ended up taking them nowhere. We call it twenty-twenty hindsight. We don't have that in the freak-out, only after.

The same is true for us. When we're in the middle of a hard situation or uncharted territory, we do everything we can just to make it through it. We can have times of laughter, as the pioneers did at the campfire, but oftentimes what we're experiencing is the underlying tension of change. The hardest part about uncharted territory is that we try our best and only when we get to the end can we see what mistakes or triumphs we made along the way. When we are marching forward, just like the pioneers, we can see what is in front of us, what is on the horizon. If we cannot see beyond the horizon, we rely on faith.

Our only fallback is the way things once were. But in the freak-out place, what once was is being replaced by what is coming.

COOKIES BEFORE, COOKIES AFTER

In the beginning of my family's celiac-disease journey, I desperately wanted them to know that eating gluten free would be okay. I worked to make our favorites, tried to substitute what we couldn't have with what we could have. For the most part I succeeded, until we faced a gluten-free speed bump.

Christmas cookies.

Don't laugh that my giant freak-out moment was because of Christmas cookies. In my family, Grandma Laurella, my dad's mom, made the most amazing cookies at Christmastime. She would spend weeks prepping them, decorating them, getting them ready for us to eat on Christmas Eve. In fact, I don't remember most gifts my grandparents gave me, but I absolutely remember those Moravian gingerbread cookies.

A week before my second child, Chloé, was born, my grandmother died. My family knew how much my grandma meant to me, and several weeks after her death, they gave me a box that held my grandma's cookie cutters. All of them. The stars, the snowflakes, the trees. The box was a priceless gift capturing memories and ensuring that Christmas-cookie making continued on our family's timeline.

When those cookie cutters came home to my house, I felt as if the gift of cookies was being passed down to me. As a result, despite the tremendous mess, cookie making at Christmastime became part of our family's tradition.

And then, after Samuel's diagnosis, I could no longer use the main ingredient: wheat.

That first Christmas was rough. I think I cried more that year in the flour section than anyone thought possible. No matter how meticulously I followed my grandma's cookie recipes (sans the wheat flour), the cookies still came out of my oven messed up. Flat, burnt, tasting of strange bean flours. I would try, would ruin another batch, and would try again.

One night after seeing my grandma's favorite gingerbread cookies come out flat and without the star and tree shapes, I called my friend Amy.

"I just want to quit. This is so unfair! Amy, I hate this part," I said, sobbing into the phone. I wanted to make them so badly, wanted what I remembered, wanted my kids to have the gift of what I remembered, and I wasn't getting anywhere but angry.

Amy listened, understood the freak-out, knew I needed the freedom to grieve what once was. But then when the time was right, she changed my perspective. She said, "Rach, sometimes you have to let go. You can't stay in the past making cookies you used to love. You have to forge ahead and create new traditions. Find a new gluten-free Christmas cookie recipe your family will love. And make that the tradition. Be happy for the other cookie years and know that you will soon be just as happy with the new gluten-free years."

I kept making cookies. Year after year.

And this year, Chloé, who has my grandma's name as her middle name, stood in my house in Tennessee, rolling pin in hand, rolling out gluten-free dough and pressing her namesake's cookie cutters in the gingerbread.

When I was in the middle of the freak-out space, with bags of flours around and messed-up cookies, I didn't know there would be that December day in Tennessee with Chloé yelling, "Sam! Cookies are ready!," and him running to get one and then immediately asking for another. But I can proudly tell you that I've now mastered making a gluten-free Moravian gingerbread cookie that would make my sweet grandma beam with pride.

I'm sure those pioneers had some great recipes they carried with them. Just because those folks were in the unknown didn't mean birthdays and traditions didn't continue. The world's calendar doesn't stop flipping when we are going through transitions.

They, too, had to make the choice to love what once was and also embrace what they could do in the moment. The other cool thing? I don't fully remember my Grandma's cookies anymore. I know I loved them. But I do remember and love the new cookies we made this winter. And judging by the empty cookie tin, so does everyone else.

When you are in your own space of change, you need to understand several things: it is okay to feel freaked out (remember my friend Amy's words), you will make it through, and you will find joy on the other side.

March Forward

When you are in the freak-out spaces, it often feels as though you are living in and dealing with both spaces—the previous patterns and cycles of the past as well as the new normal you're working on establishing. As you make changes, you will find yourself needing to let go of the past and be willing to create a new future. Think back to chapter 10 and my drama with the dining room table and dinners. Beyond showing how I had to let go of perfectionism, the story also illustrates how perfectionism should not be used in the freak-outs of life. In order to move forward, I had to be willing to march from what once was.

We can't just hit Delete on the previous patterns and realities of life. If we could, we would never get stuck, being afraid to let go of the past, and we would never have the freak-out space meaning we were trying to better our lives. Instead, we are forced to live in the uncomfortableness of change. This means we also deal with the emotional-baggage excuse. Again, think of the pioneers. Do you know what new pioneers would see on the edge of the trail? Stuff. Chairs and tables and that beautiful heirloom cabinet. The pioneers were forced to lighten the load, and in that space, lightening the load meant letting go of what they once deemed priceless and irreplaceable.

That's the process of moving forward in the freak-out spaces. You have to let go. You are going to change and then have to wait while the change takes effect. The patterns and normal need to settle into a new normal.

I didn't just magically pay off every creditor the day I transformed my thinking. The IRS didn't back down saying, "Sweet! We'll erase your debt because you have a new mindset." Instead, paying off debts has been a process of months and years of incremental change. I'm not even done yet, but I'm making progress, and I'm much closer to the end than if I had continued to bury my head in the sand, ignoring it. In the same way, it took seven years to figure out how to make those cookies. Seven years of trial and error, but in it all, movement forward.

You have to march onward, even when you are in the freak-out, believing that *every single day* is another step toward wholeness. Remember, the longer you have resided in an old cycle and process of thinking, the more resistance you will experience in the changing. This means you might have moments of calling friends, panicked about your life, hoping it becomes chill once again. It also means you might feel as if you're stumbling a whole lot, such as in cookie-flop times. But with each waver, you stand up again, having learned what made you stumble, and thus you become wiser.

As hard as it might seem, that freak-out space is not a bad place. There's no shame for residing in that spot. You are being human. And you need to understand that when you are in the midst of a doubt place, that *does not mean* you are turning back.

In fact, congratulations for being in a freak-out space. It means you took a risk, decided to step out, and broke a cycle. And if you broke a cycle, it means you are moving to a new reality, a new place, a new dream, a new normal.

See that goal.

Tell your friends about it too.

And breathe.

16

Don't Do Life and Dreams Alone—Armor Up!

We were not created and expected to do life alone, as if we were plopped on this earth in an isolated bubble. The moment my first child, Hannah, was placed in my arms became a moment my heart was forever linked to another person. My mother felt the same. And her mother. And her mother. And all of us, no matter how much motherhood feels like a solo endeavor, know that we need someone to call with all those questions of "Will this be okay?" This journey of motherhood, this walk to find significance, this brave art of change, was never meant to be walked alone.

Think again about my favorite brave historical people, those pioneers. They didn't set out to Oregon by themselves, but rather they traveled with a group of equally hopeful individuals. Those moms on that trip didn't just leave child rearing and child watching to only their own wagon; they worked together to keep the entire party safe. At night they didn't leave their wagons open but instead circled them, making a strong force of unity, not individuality. When I was in my low moment in San Diego, my church friends didn't leave me, fending for myself; they circled around me, protecting me, believing me, helping me.

The motto of friendship needs to be this: we don't just stay there in the stuck with one another; we keep moving forward, believing in one another.

Think about your moments of great accomplishment, great joy. Do you know what makes them powerful? It's that friend on the other side of the finish line cheering you on, just as excited as you are, wiping the tears from your eyes and telling you, "I always knew you could do it!" Think about how much of a gift that friend is and how much of a gift it is to *be* that friend.

Don't try to do this journey alone.

When we open our lives to our friends, we share a collective story. You don't hear much about a pioneer, but you do hear about the pioneers—the group.

I don't know if you can see it throughout each chapter, but there was rarely a moment when I made any change completely on my own. Oh yes, the middle-of-the-night resolve was certainly my strength. But in the moments of doubt, I had so many others, whether I realized it initially or not, who loved me so much that they stepped in and held me up when I grew tired. They reminded me about truths—about my purpose, my calling, my abilities.

If we are going to be a generation of moms striving to be who we were created to be, we cannot venture on this journey on our own, thinking that we can do this alone. Strengthening, encouraging, and even challenging one another is what we must bravely do. We need to set down our masks, our fears, and open our doors to others in our lives. And we need to be the ones who believe in others and remind *them* of their bravery as well.

This is the charge of friendship.

FRIENDS ARMOR UP WITH YOU

In the six months prior to Samuel being diagnosed with celiac disease, I observed him waste away in front of me. Oh, he faded, and he faded hard. He stopped eating, lost weight, would scream in pain when he'd try to go to the bathroom, would sleep all the time, and lost that zest for life. I tried to reassure myself that it wasn't that bad, but deep down I knew something was terribly wrong.

Seeing your child suffer creates a fight like no other, a fight we all have inside, a fight—shown in the survival strength—that we instantly have access to. During those months, I spent hours online reading medical journals, Googling symptoms, scouring forums, and I even spent more hours visiting clinics and calling doctors in a desperate attempt to save my sweet Sammy boy. But searching for the clichéd needle in a haystack was maddening. And having doctors tell me he was fine was even more discouraging.

Finally, my friend Amy (from the cookie story) could clearly see Sam's decline and no longer stayed an encouraging friend but became the "armored up" friend and joined my battle. To armor up means you don't sit on the sidelines of your friend's life but rather band together, knowing it might be a fight and being willing to accept the gashes that happen during battle. When a friend invests the same level of ownership with the problem that you do, that's when you really get stuff done.

When Amy started to fight, she got her father-in-law, an emergency room physician, involved. He lived several hundred miles from us but called a pediatrician in my then-hometown of Minneapolis. This local pediatrician became concerned. She didn't want us to wait for an appointment; she asked us to march into the hospital immediately because she, too, feared for his life.

Sam and I didn't go to the emergency room alone.

Amy kept fighting, kept holding my hand, kept prodding me forward. And she marched into the Minneapolis Children's Hospital emergency room with me. On that very cold January day, as we went through the sliding doors into the colorful waiting room, she whispered, "There's no turning back now. Let's save Sam."

We walked to the front desk and were instantly sent to the triage room. As I spoke to the nurse, describing in detail my worry while my sixteen-month-old slept in my arms, Amy gave me the smile of courage and added in critical details I dismissed. Amy had clarity; she was fresh in the fight; she spoke up. She could see that the fragments of the story mattered.

Three days later, in order to be diagnosed with celiac disease, Samuel needed an intestinal biopsy. Despite it being another day spent in the hospital, this time in the surgical suite, Amy never left. Amy's father-in-law stayed invested. Sam's new pediatrician, whom I knew only through one phone call, was the one now listed as his pediatrician. To save Sam's life, we needed the biopsy results. There is something very raw in the moments before you send your child to an operating room to be put under anesthesia. You know it is right, it is what is needed, but the reality of letting your child go, of his or her life being in the hand of another, can be heartbreaking.

Amy felt it too. And as the nurse came to get Sam and me to take us to the operating room, Amy, despite the tears in her own eyes, looked in my eyes and said, "You've got this, Rach. You can do it."

We both felt the hurt. We both knew we needed to be strong. We encouraged and strengthened each other. Sam may have been *my* son, but he was my fight as well as Amy's. She knew how much I hurt and how strong I needed to be for him. Her words weren't pity but were the words that warriors shout before battle.

I carried Samuel in my arms, next to the nurse, down the long hallway, past other families waiting, into the blinding lights of the operating room. So many people were looking at us when we entered, so many faces of concern. There was no waiting, no pausing, no instances of me saying, "I changed my mind." Instead, as I laid Samuel on the table, I happened to glance at the computer where I saw his name, Samuel J. Martin, in bold letters. In that moment, the fear was replaced with deep peace. Everyone in that room was there for my precious Sam.

The fight, because Amy stepped in, was now an army.

The anesthesiologist let me lean next to Samuel as he lowered the mask to his little face. I whispered to Sam about how brave he was and how I loved him and how he would be okay. I spoke truth to not just him but also myself.

We all were helping him find life again. Amy was right: I could handle this.

I fought the right fight. I didn't stop walking down the hallway to the operating room. I didn't about-face once I entered. I didn't panic. I didn't fight the mask that put him under. And I didn't stay when they told me I needed to leave.

I trusted them. We were a team.

So many people have told me how strong I was during those days. You know what? I *was* strong. That was a test of strength, of never accepting an excuse. But I wasn't strong because of me alone; I was strong because of my friend's support. Amy was the friend who donned the armor to join me and wouldn't back down in the moments of doubt.

After Sam's surgery, I walked out of the operating room and found Amy still there, waiting for me. She looked at me, walked over, and held me. "I am so proud of you," she told me. "He will be okay."

Your charge? To be the friend who steps in instead of looking away.

FRIENDS IGNORE YOUR EXCUSES

For years I had shut the door to my world so tightly that I didn't know how to see the people who were there for me. But they were there. I just needed to open my life enough to allow them in. It was a process of letting go of my excuse of pride that hid the dysfunction and unhappiness behind the closed front door. But the more I dropped that isolating bag-gage, the more I realized I was never alone.

My friend Maria is my soul-sister friend from Minnesota. When my family and I first moved into our home there, I remember seeing her in the backyard, weeding her grass. She was doing life, a life in that moment when we were two strangers, neither of us aware that one day we would be best friends. As the years passed, the line between our yards blurred and instead of it being just her in the backyard, it became us working side by side. Each of us moved from being the woman who lived behind another to the friend who was always around. Maria and I would spend hours sitting in the grass between our two homes, watching the kids play, still picking at those weeds, and just being there for each other in all the moments in between.

When life fragmented around me, when I moved from being the married friend to the single friend, from the stay-at-home mom to the working mom, she didn't back off. She did the opposite. She didn't judge—she loved. She was present, always watching, always ready to walk across the yard and into my home. She didn't change her friendship with me based on the state of my house or the dollars in my checkbook or the anxiety I dealt with.

In fact, there were many days when Maria would show up at my door with a bucket of cleaning supplies in her hand and walk right in. The meet-friends-on-the-porch rule didn't apply to Maria. She knew how hard it was for me to ask for help in those years, she knew I was full of ex-cuses, so she did what friends do: she showed up. Sometimes she'd arrive with a latte for me to drink. Other times she'd take my boys to get their hair cut because I was working. Some afternoons she'd be out back mow-ing my yard and picking the weeds. There were days when she would get just "a few" groceries for me. And many times she would just sit with me and listen while tears fell.

She never stopped being there, and I know, even now as I write this almost nine hundred miles away from her, she is still there for me.

One January day, in the first months after my divorce, I reached my breaking point. I was still deep in financial woes and was unable to continue homeschooling my kids because I was now the family's bread-winner. Homeschooling had been all I'd known, all I had ever done as a parent, and when I had to quit that, part of me felt that I'd failed. I had forged my identity around that type of education, and now I was waving the white flag of surrender. And I was also terrified. The school had called and needed some test scores from my kids that the state required each year. Those tests? I wanted the kids to take them, I planned on them, but when I asked for the funds for them, I was told the money wasn't there. As a result I lived in fear.

Now I was dealing with the results: the ripple.

I admitted to Maria that not only did I need help but also I had, in fact, stumbled greatly in not figuring out a way, despite what I was told, to have the kids take those tests. It was so hard to admit this to Maria because she is a teacher. My shame felt so heavy, so insurmountable. Maria didn't see the shame; she saw what needed to be done. So one day, dressed to go outside in the subzero temps, she picked me up in her car and drove me to the kids' new school. Then she walked me, the friend in need of support, into the principal's office. As we sat together in the room waiting, my body trembled in fear.

Maria put her hand on my shoulder and said, "It will be okay."

Those are the words of friendship—not passive, dismissive, judg-mental words but words that express things will be all right because that friend isn't giving up on you.

Maria ignored my excuses. Instead, she pushed me to come face to face with my fears and do what was right. She didn't run from my past's ripple and didn't want me to either.

With her next to me, I shared my fears and lack of test scores with the principal.

After I came clean, Principal Aanerud looked at me and said, "Oh, Rachel, your kids will be just fine. You are brave and doing a wonderful thing today! I'm so thankful you trusted us enough to love your kids. I promise you, we won't let you down. We don't care about the past, just today."

I faced my fears and received grace from the principal, but I didn't get there without Maria.

I never would have been given that moment in the principal's office if I hadn't had the courage Maria cemented within me. Because of that courage, when we walked together into that principal's office, I was bravely able to say, "Please help."

Good friends make that relationship a priority, good friends call each other out when needed, good friends show up for each other, and good friends ignore your excuses. I had so many reasons for why public school wouldn't be good for my kids or how I'd messed up, but Maria loved me beyond them.

In fact, remember the weeds in the yard? They became our battle together. No neighbor-role excuses. Not a "her yard, my yard" battle but an "our yard" one. And that? That's what friends do.

FRIENDS SUPPORT YOUR DREAMS

Several years ago I started a business called Blogging Concentrated with my friend Dan. You might remember him from the dinnertime perfection story. Our company teaches and trains entrepreneurs, bloggers, and creators how to take an idea and make it a reality. In some ways, we help others get unstuck. We travel, put on workshops, speak as keynotes, and work with clients who want to understand the details, steps, and vision for making their dreams come to fruition. During part of our company's growth, I was going through my divorce as well as my own personal struggles and trials. I was dealing not only with my new role as single mom but also with stepping back into the world as a working woman. Most of my emotions were in tumble-dry mode, flipping over and over, finding nowhere safe to rest.

Though I should have been thrilled by how well my career and business were going, I still wrestled with doubt regarding my capabilities, knowledge, and ability to be taken seriously in this competitive world. One evening, after presenting our eight-hour workshop in Seattle, I was completely exhausted emotionally. Dan and I stopped at a Walgreens before heading to our client dinner, and as we pulled into the parking lot, I told him, "Thank you so much for choosing me to be your business partner. I know I'm lucky since there are so many vying to be in the spot I'm in. So thank you. I'm truly humbled."

He bristled a bit and then told me never to say that to him again.

I was shocked. I thought I was just being grateful.

Dan, however, didn't agree with or like my statement because he knew I was doubting myself. He told me, "You know what? You need to ignore everyone out there who is not believing in you. You need to be stronger than all of them. I want the word on the street to be, 'How did Dan get so lucky to have Rachel from *Finding Joy* agree to be his business partner?' If you were the president of Yahoo!, that's what they'd be saying. So no more of this grateful stuff about me choosing you. Start acting like you are as confident as the Yahoo! CEO is."

I was mad. So mad I would have stormed out of that car, except we were in the middle of Seattle.

"How can you say that to me?" I asked him. "Don't you know how hard my life is? Don't you know I was thanking you for the opportunity you gave?" I didn't like that he'd called me out on my confidence.

He knew that for me to stand up to critics and competitors, I needed to be willing to stand in front of a roomful of people and have the courage to be proud of myself. He knew that I needed to stop seeing my success as someone else giving me an opportunity but rather as my working hard and creating a company. He knew, despite the bracelet from Haiti on my wrist, those words were some unchallenged target statements that still defined me as a victim. And as the victim, I was looking to other people to either save me or have power over me.

Dan did neither of those things. He was my friend and he believed in me. Just as Dan told me, I'm telling you: You need to surround yourself with people who believe in you more than you believe in yourself, people who will force you to live out your value. You need people who will make you rise to the expectations they see in you because we all need motivation—no matter how strong we are. Friends who motivate you to be better make you better.

This is what you need to do for your friends. When you hear them doubting themselves or questioning opportunities, it is your calling, your job, to be the one who says, "Knock it off. I know it's hard, but you are doubting the awesomeness of you. You can do this—I believe in you."

FRIENDS DON'T HAVE A TIMETABLE

Our home in Minneapolis was about one hour from the airport. When I first started speaking nationwide, I still had the ripple of money issues. Therefore, something as simple as getting to the airport became filled with complications because the logistics threatened to derail my intent. If I drove to the airport, I would have to park my vehicle for the days I was gone, and that could cost me sixty to a hundred dollars each time. And back then, I just didn't have the extra money.

My friends knew this. My friend Lori? She is my friend who never let a timetable stop her from being there. She would show up at my door when I needed her and cut and color my hair every six weeks. And she became the friend who would pick me up outside my home at 3:15 a.m. to take me to the airport. When I'd open the door, she never complained about the hour but would instead hand me a cup of freshly brewed coffee and tell me how excited she was to be there. Never a frown, just a smile.

She would drive me the hour to the airport and then an hour back and then to work.

During these airport runs, I'd get in the car, feeling guilty about the early hour, and Lori would tell me, "I am so thankful for these times with you, Rachel. I get to hear about your life. This time is my favorite." She would minister to me, in the way friends do, and encourage me trip after trip. When we would get to the airport, she would always tell me, "Don't be afraid. I'm proud of you. I'll be here waiting when you get back." Time after time my plane would land and there she would be, in the passenger pickup line, waiting for me to load my luggage into the back.

Lori didn't have an "I'm a friend during these hours only" timetable. She gave her time because she believed in me. She could see that what I needed was time and a friend, and in those days of her life, she sacrificed her time for me.

One of the greatest things we can do as friends is give up our time for each other. There will be afternoons when your friends just need you to listen. There will be days when you can pick up their kids so they can get to work. What if you are great at math and your friend's child is struggling? Could you give your time there?

Be the person who is labeled "3 a.m. Friend" on your friend's phone.

Do the hard things. Be the village.

Hidden Friends Around You

I know you may struggle with feeling alone and are convinced that friends are not really there. But is it possible friends are knocking on your door and you just don't see them? I bet there is someone who is trying or has tried and you missed it. It might be the barista at Starbucks who always knows your name or your neighbor who waves at you when you pick up your kids. It might be the mom at preschool who talks with you day after day. What happened to walking over and simply saying hello without all the expectations of being put together? You may have potential friends who are just waiting for you to say yes to friendship.

Saying yes is such a powerful friendship tool because it opens doors and breaks down boundaries and exposes excuses. Think about the times you have helped your friends. Did it make you feel good? Why not give them the same gift and allow them to help you? You'll both benefit. Truthfully, there are people placed in our lives, but often we just need to wake up and see them.

For ten years while I lived in Minnesota, my church friend Jen showed up for me. She would watch my kids and invite them over. She gave and gave, yet I didn't realize the depth of her friendship until after I moved away. It makes me teary to write those words, so humbled, because all the times when I would say I felt alone, Jen was always there.

When it was time for me to move my family to Nashville, on a cold Minnesota winter day as the world prepped for Christmas, Jen and her entire family pulled up to my house, got out, and helped carry everything I owned to the moving truck. Box after box after box. Anytime I would apologize for them having to be there right before Christmas, Jen would look at me and say, "This is exactly where we are supposed to be today."

She showed up. She demonstrated true friendship.

Who are you missing in your life who is ready to become that kind of friend to you? Who can you be that friend to?

Open your eyes and look around. Someone is there, waiting for you.

FRIENDSHIP GOES BOTH WAYS

Here is where we get to the most important part of this book. Even though my words might seem to be just about your personal change, your finding self again, your bravery, your fight against fear and finding happiness, it goes so much deeper. This journey, this story, is not yours alone anymore.

So I am bestowing on you a charge.

A calling.

And that is to be the friend to another that you need for yourself.

As someone helps you, remember that you can be a friend as well. You are going to have friends who will desperately need you to armor up for them. They might not even know how to verbalize it to you. But here's the most powerful way to know if you need to join the battle. If you find yourself saying to a friend or an acquaintance, "You are so strong. I could never do what you can do," then that is your calling and your charge to see where you can become the friend who helps that mom breathe.

Do not exempt yourself from action. Armor up.

I want us to be the kind of friend Maria was to me. I want us to see through our friends' excuses. We need to be the friends who don't accept someone just meeting us at the front door and keeping us there. We need to be the friends who, like Maria, come with the bucket of supplies and walk in. This means we listen to our friends' fears, but instead of letting them stall momentum, we help debunk the excuses so they can move forward. That's part of bravery.

This is what you need to do for your friends too. When you hear them identify themselves by the dot labels the world slaps on them, it is your job to call out those labels and help them remove them. Don't sit by and let them doubt themselves; be the person who challenges them to rise to the expectations. Be their cheerleader and dot remover.

An interesting thing happens when you give of yourself for your friends: you rediscover purpose and renew strength. My friend Amy, from the celiac disease story, blessed me in that way when I was able to be the one to show up with my time. When her family was moving from Minneapolis to Pittsburgh, I originally was just planning to help load the van (and shed all those tears because my friend was moving across the country). But as soon as I arrived, I could see that the moving truck they rented was too small. They needed another vehicle—and another driver.

I didn't hesitate. I volunteered.

I found someone to watch my kids for two and a half days, packed a bag, finished loading their boxes, and drove through the night to Pittsburgh. I followed their van for mile after mile after mile and felt such a deep purpose of authentic gratitude. I was thankful for *my* gift of time, my turn to give back to our collective friendship.

Friends give of time. We don't just take, take, take; we give as well. Remember the pioneers: they gave to one another so they *all* could make it.

YOUR CHARGE

Sometimes when I go through the drive-through at Starbucks, the barista at the window will tell me, "The person in front of you paid for you. It's your lucky day!" It's always the coolest thing, this moment when someone stepped out of his or her own busy timeline to affect someone else's. It's also in that moment when I have a choice: accept the gift or extend the ripple.

"I'll pay for the car behind me," I say back.

That's extending the ripple. The best part of paying for the car behind me is that when I pull away from the drive-through window, I know that others will experience kindness in their world. I don't expect them to pay it forward, but I do hope that they, in the midst of whatever cycle or journey they are on, know that someone else in this world thought of them.

That is friendship.

Remember, the first step to having a friend is being one. Friendship is rarely convenient. Look at every story from my life: those friends inconvenienced themselves because of love. That's what makes friendship so powerful. Think of your friends. How would they rate you as their friend? What would it require for them to call you the "best friend a person could have"? What would it take for them to write about you in a book? You might need to show up on the doorstep of a friend's house. In fact, I challenge you to do that. Move beyond just a Facebook like to a phone call or a time sitting across from each other at the coffee shop on days other than regularly scheduled.

Think of it as a dare, the art of living out of bravery, and decide to no longer just be the mom in the line but the mom who is the friend.

You can't do life without friends, and that means you must take responsibility to be there for them, just as my sweetest friends have for me.

When we share our lives with our friends, our dreams are given greater meaning. All those pioneers relied on their friends in the next wagon to reinforce the victory of crossing into Oregon.

Friends help us move bravely forward.

Fight for your heart, jump into the pool, volunteer, write, fulfill your dreams, venture on a mission trip, but sweet, sweet sister, don't do it alone.

Run the race together.

17

It's Your Story—Own It

After moving to a new place, especially when you have kids, you are faced with a ridiculous amount of paperwork. You would think that in this digital age we could save some trees, yet after I moved, I found myself with stacks of paper in front of me. Most of the forms had boxes to check about my marital status: married, single, divorced, remarried, widowed. Checking the "divorced" box filled me with shame. I didn't want to mark "divorced." Why couldn't I just check "single"? Then I became irritated that anyone needed to know my relationship status. Did it really matter to the doctor discussing my anemia with me that I was divorced? Did my dentist think the extra plaque was the result of that "divorced" box being checked?

One day while filling out yet another form with the marital-status boxes, I realized I should be confident in checking "divorced." Anything else would mean I wasn't owning my story. If I hadn't marked "divorced," I wouldn't be filling out that paperwork in Tennessee. It would mean I never had done the hard things, never had journeyed through the freak-out, never had found joy and normal again. Having ventured through that part of my life, while painful and hard, is my story. And I needed to own not just the cool and wonderful parts but all of it—challenges too. My story meant I was married for seventeen years, had seven kids, and went through bankruptcy and dealt with the IRS, but it also meant I learned a lot of lessons, built a successful blog and business, and experienced life. So now I unashamedly check that box because it is the whole truth of me.

You need to own your story too. All the parts: good and bad, happy and crazy, fearful and focused. The grand parts and the parts that cover you with fear and shame and regret. The next phase of your life doesn't have to be a retelling of the first. And there's a good chance that the lessons from the first will influence the impact of your remaining days.

I live today aware of the dreams, goals, and possibilities for my family and friends.

I also live today diligent to my own heart's passion.

Checking that box in the pediatrician's office in Nashville meant I had done it. I'd made the journey. It might not be Oregon, but it was my own trail. And in that moment, there was no shame, only healthy accomplishment. I was proud of my story.

As you pursue the brave art of motherhood, navigating all the joys and sorrows, dreams and unmet expectations, you, too, will have to own your story.

In fact, I want you to own your story.

Because you matter. And your story is part of you.

"What Would Awesome You Do?"

One winter several years ago, at a blogging conference I was speaking at in Toronto, one of the other sessions caught my eye: "What Would Awesome You Do?" Even though I was tired to my bones from the day's full events and desperately wanted to trek back to my hotel room to get a needed hour of sleep, I grabbed more coffee and willed myself to sit in on the session.

I'm glad I did. The speaker, Nicole Dean, asked a series of questions designed to knock off any minimizing doubt we carry around about ourselves and to help us see our potential clearly. She queried those in the room, "If you had a superhero self called 'Awesome You,' how would you be different?"

As she spoke, I heard, *Is this what awesome Rachel would do?*

Ed had asked me something similar years before. When he pushed me to have faith in a future reality, he also challenged me to have faith to visualize a different me in my timeline's future. Sometimes it is difficult to create a vision of ourselves when we're mired in the present. If you can't imagine Awesome You at the moment, can you instead visualize you in ten years if your dreams and future plans work out?

I know it may be strange, but here's the truth. Most people might decide that it's too strange to envision themselves in the future, and because they don't want to be different, they agree to be like everyone else. They skip this step. *Do not* skip this part.

A figure skater visualizes her entire routine thousands of times, every edge of the skates, every turn, all the jumps. She goes over it in her head until her visualization is flawless. She imagines the coolness of the air, hears the sound of her skates scraping the ice, tastes the sweat on her upper lip, feels the burn in her legs, experiences the impact of landing on one skate, hears the roar of the crowd. The more details, the more powerful.

She doesn't visualize falling—she visualizes landing after the jump. She doesn't visualize a moment now but a moment in the future.

What you need to do is no different from what figure skaters do.

I want you to really think about the person you will become:

- Do you live as though you are awesome and have every answer at your fingertips?
- In what ways would your life look different from how it looks now?
- Would you be afraid to make that phone call? Start your dream? Lose the weight? Write?

- Why are you not living that way now? What holds you back from being your Awesome You?
- If you know that your Awesome You would not be afraid, why aren't you living that way now?

Living out of your Awesome You places means living without the excuses but with potential.

What would your Awesome You be?

Start living out of that paradigm, being confident in that future, and you will open yourself up to opportunities you didn't see before.

DON'T BE SCARED OF BEING CONFIDENT

America's Got Talent is one of my family's favorite television shows. My kids love the acts, and I love the stories about each person trying out. More often than not, the stories highlight the underdog. In the summer of 2017, as part of his act, a magician (our family's favorite kind of performer) asked Mel B, one of the judges, to think of one word that describes herself.

"Goddess," she answered without hesitating.

I don't remember the rest of the magic act, but I do remember her response. It was an instantaneous, without-a-doubt, cemented-in-her-mind description of who she believed herself to be. Whether or not you agree with her assessment, you need to understand the confidence of self it takes to give that answer. She wasn't pretending, wasn't dealing with the voices in her head telling her not to say it; rather she embraced, well, herself.

To be fully transparent, if I ever happened to be on national television and was asked to describe myself, I'm sure I wouldn't answer immediately. I probably would wrestle with my doubts and my worries about what others would think and then deliver a "safe" answer.

Calling oneself a goddess is the furthest thing from safe.

It's bold, confident, and daring.

I don't want a safe life—I want that confidence. Do you too?

There are times, though, when that kind of confidence scares us. Have you ever been in a room where there is that confident woman, and then in the back of the room, a group of women say, "Ha. Who does she think she is?" We know it happens, that talk behind the scenes, that attempt to bust confidence. It can be painful, stifling, but you have to ask yourself, *Would I rather be the one with confidence and happiness or the one in the back of the room cutting down someone for her confidence?* I'm not saying you'd be petty, but what I am absolutely saying is that you have to have such a strong confidence that it doesn't crumble when the critics are loose.

Mel B has critics. She has a public life in which the details—her divorce, family structure, day-to-day actions—are fair game for discussion. She didn't care. She called herself a goddess.

If you were on that stage and were asked to describe yourself, what would you say?

It takes courage to be that confident. It's okay for us to be confident in who we are and who we are called to be. It's okay to be that confident, just like Mel B, when our life stories don't belong on the Hallmark Channel. And more than being okay, it's a powerful moment when the true confidence in you in the moment—as a mom and as a woman—is allowed to shine.

THE STORY IN BETWEEN

I have become good friends with the baristas at my local coffee shop during this book-writing experience. The other day, as I grabbed my caramel macchiato, my barista friend Emilee asked about this book, so I told her about the impending due date and thus my need for the extra shot of espresso. Then out of the blue, I said, "You know, you can't write the end until you know the beginning, but what you *really* need to know is the story in between."

She told me to put the "in between" reference in the book.

She's right.

The story in between is *your* story.

Do you want to know what the brave art of motherhood really is?

It's the in between. It's your whole story, with the ups and downs and cycles broken and lessons learned. It's the agreements. It's the times when you never, never, never, *never* give up and the times when you start over. It's all the days, the weeks, the months that your calendar flips through. It's not the final destination. It's not point B on the journey. It's your *now*.

This is why I believe that no matter where you start, you can live a life of exponential potential, with greater possibilities and vibrant dreams. Don't think, *I could never do that,* when you read about someone else's success. Instead, from this day forward, challenge yourself to think, *What if I tried?* It's a dare to put one foot in front of the other, to march on, to have faith in your capabilities and future, and unwaveringly understand that you are worth living a life of vibrancy, meaning, and joy.

Your life matters, and you are worth believing in yourself. You are worth daring to have faith and hope again. You are worth rightly ordered relationships. You are worth having and pursuing dreams. You are worth being loving and being loved. You are worth a life with a variety of stories you can one day laugh about and cry over.

When Grandma Laurella held my daughter Hannah the first time, she looked at me and said, "It feels like yesterday that this was your dad. It goes fast. Don't worry about the mistakes. Just live with joy. Live alive." And that? That's what I want you to remember.

You are worth a life vibrantly alive.

18

Cross to the Other Side

The first spring break after moving to Nashville and getting a second start, we drove from Tennessee through Alabama until we got to the Gulf of Mexico. My kids sat in our van, a van I completely owned, excited about this new adventure. We stopped for gas, I paid for it without worrying about my card getting declined, and then at lunch I let them order whatever they wanted instead of sharing. My bills were paid, opportunities were on the horizon, and this book was moving from being just a thought to actually being put on paper.

I drove mile after mile, but this time not to start a new life or save one of my children. This time I drove because I had in my life what I'd never had before: margin. I no longer had the pressures of finances choking out opportunity or the loss of self and identity.

And in that margin between busy and expectations, I held a secret: freedom. It was the freedom to tell my children to find the suitcases tucked in closets in our new home, pack them with their clothes, and hop in the van. They didn't witness me fretting; they saw me eager and with deep undeniable happiness.

That day, we drove and drove until the road ran out and the Gulf stood in front of us.

We all tumbled out—a big pile of us, tired from sitting in the van for eight hours. And as my kids got out, their senses awoke to the salty sea's smell. As the orange sun set, they sprinted across the white sand to the edge of the land—the meeting of earth and sea—took off their shoes, and for the first time ever experienced the majesty of the ocean.

It was magical.

There in front of me were my children living the results of bravery. Their clothes were heavy with salt water, and their laughter and screams of delight echoed with the crash of the surf.

It didn't matter that it was unseasonably cold that night. It didn't matter that the beach was almost empty. It didn't matter that we were hungry. None of those reasons to step away from the water mattered because in that moment it became about life. Life in its most basic, beautiful, and joyous form. Life with moments, with experiences, with family. Life with freedom.

As I basked in the sacredness of that moment, the realization washed over me.

This is the other side.

We were no longer stuck in the cycle. We had made it out. I wasn't a slave to excuses—I had opportunities. I stood there not as a fragmented person but as someone who loved the entirety of who I was created to be. As the Alabama sun set and my children freely jumped in the water, I knew that all the dreams, hard work, and pushing myself to the edge of myself mattered. No longer was "Take my kids to the ocean" an item on a bucket list, as it had been for twenty years. Instead, it became an item that, when I got home, I proudly crossed off.

Bravery.

Those events, those checking-off-the-list moments, are the beautiful, powerful, and profound gifts on our timeline. Not just because of the moment or the absolute glory of reaching the apex but because of the deep sense, the art, of making it to that once seemingly impossible reality.

I watch my kids now in our house, oblivious, in a way, to the depth of the struggle it took to get to this place of normal. It's so simple today. I can get my kids ready for public school each morning with gluten-free packed lunches and school-lunch accounts full. My bills all have the word *paid* written on them with a circle around it. My house is clean—well, as clean as it can be with five kids still living there—and I have no qualms opening my garage door wide when the kids get home. The rain is falling, the dishwasher humming, my kids playing in the other room, and there's me sitting in front of a computer screen thinking about what I will remember if I get to fulfill my invincible dream that I'll live to be eighty-two years old.

My word, friends, I love my life.

All of it.

Even those years when I was so lost, so messed up, so hurting, because they have led me to this exact moment, this exact second of time.

Inhale, exhale. That breath is your breath of opportunity.

These are the moments you have left, the moments of choice and decision. You will continue to experience instances of falling down and standing up, but from this point on, they can be when you decide to embrace the timeline and dare to suck the marrow out of your life. Do you want to know what the brave art of motherhood really is?

It is right now.

It's not the final destination, not the end, but rather all the times you keep running, keep pressing after the goals, keep being the friend, keep showing up for your kids, keep having faith in the future.

Don't decide to be one of those people who goes to the motivational speech and leaves thinking it's awesome but walks out thinking, *That's nice—I'll do it tomorrow.* I didn't arrive at the Gulf of Mexico with my kids by believing, *We'll do it tomorrow.*

This is the only time in your entire existence when you get to live with that pinnacle choice. Decide to tolerate life or change life. Decide to give up the inch or fight for the inch. Decide to listen to the excuses or break the excuses. Decide to doubt or have faith. Decide to live by the target or reframe the target. Decide to stay the same or change.

You can decide now, right in your in-between place on your timeline.

Years ago, that is what my counselor, Ed, wanted. He wanted me to choose the path of faith.

You no longer have to live on hold. When you die, the choice is gone—the choice to live and follow dreams or the choice to sit in fear. This moment, this day, is when you can look at your talents and decide, *Today is the day*. When I looked at my life, at the timeline scratched on butcher paper, I realized there was a moment when I anchored my future, drove a stake in the ground, and determined, without wavering, *Today is my day*.

Today is your day.

Remember you. Celebrate your story. Show up and try.

Live a life without excuses. Live with hope. Live with determination. Live with joy. Love your kids. Be a friend. Find joy. Be brave. Breathe.

And start.

That's the brave art of motherhood.

My Visual Journey

This book is without pictures. It's you and me sharing coffee, talking about life. My hope was that you would be able to focus on your life and dreams, so I thought it might be distracting to add pictures of my own.

But in the age of Instagram and iPhones, I took plenty of pictures documenting my every moment. There are images from the night at the Gulf of Mexico and pictures of me exhausted on planes. There are pictures of my van engulfed in flames and images of me being interviewed by the media regarding the fire. There are simple things too, such as lacing up my running shoes or sitting in a hospital bed pre-op. Those stories are the foundation of this book and of breaking free.

So in the event you'd like to go deeper into the stories I've written about here, you can go to my blog, *Finding Joy,* where I have created a visual journey.

I'd be honored to have you share my journey and would love to hear from you.

And yes, you'll find many pictures of me next to my coffee.

FindingJoy.net/visualjourney

Acknowledgments

I always thought these were silly—until I wrote my book. Isn't that the way life is? You make a judgment about something, and then when you're in that position, you end up realizing, *Whoa, was I wrong*. Now I grasp the importance of this section. I just do. This is the spot of thank you, of friendship, of realizing there is no way I could be me without the amazing people who loved me when I jumped into the deep water and had no idea how to swim.

My best friend, Dan R. Morris, is that person. He always believed I could do hard things way before I could see them. He was like me when I was encouraging my son Elijah to jump into the pool, but he saw how stubborn I was, and instead of waiting, he pushed me in and made me figure it out. We've had our journeys, our ups and downs. He and I own Audience Industries and have presented hundreds of our Blogging Concentrated events worldwide. You really learn to trust another person when you speak for eight hours with him or sit together while you fly to the other side of the world. I can tell you that without his faith in me, I wouldn't be who I am today. Find yourself a Dan, my friend. Life is too short not to have one. Just know that mine is taken.

My kids also deserve a whole bunch of thanks, not only for providing me with stories—some of them crazy—but also for having the patience to deal with me as I wrote this book. I'm sure their vision of book writing is different from what it was before. They've seen the long hours, asked questions about editing, cheered when I thought I was done, and then moaned when I informed them there was more work to do. I really do love all of them. I know that life hasn't been easy. I get that. But my life with them is so wonderful (except for laundry), and I couldn't imagine a day without them. They are the reason motherhood is part of this book's title.

My parents. Thanks for dealing with me as a child. I know I was moody. I hope now that I've written, you can be rewarded for the patience it takes to deal with an introspective soul. (If you also have that child who cries at stuff or seems too sensitive, bless you and know that he or she will make it through.) My mom and dad are saints. They really are: They never let me fall, they believed in me, and they had faith in what I could do. Beyond that, they provided for me during those married poverty years, gave so much, and never made me feel guilty as I worked to claw out of tough stuff. They're the best parents ever.

My siblings. Thanks, Becky, Joel, and Abby, for loving me in my worst and best, for letting me be mayor of our Lego towns we built when we were young (not that you had a choice), and for showing up for me. I'm grateful that we share our timeline of life together.

Mary and Dave Morris. Thanks for loving me like a daughter, for believing in me, and for supporting me on this up-and-down journey. You two mean the world to me. #phasetwo.

My friends. Maria, for walking into my house, for listening to everything, for showing up, for weeding the yards, and for driving with me to Tennessee. Lori, for all the haircuts and colors that really were counseling sessions and for the dozens of 3 a.m. airport treks. Amy, for being my sitting-at-the-edge-of-the-ocean-and-dreaming friend and loving me in the freak-out spaces. Dwayne, for pushing me to challenge myself and be better at basketball (game on). Jen, for always being my friend and moving all those boxes.

To the readers of *Finding Joy:* I am honestly without words for all of you. You have been my rock, my support, my sounding board. You've been with me in the ups and downs and cheered me on, and if we ever sat down in a coffee shop together, I'd have tears of joy for your friend-ship. Thanks also for rallying together and raising enough money for my family to purchase a new-to-us van after our van fire. You amaze me with your kindness.

The list. One time, on one of our flights across the country to speak, I told Dan about how I wanted to repay so many who had helped me. He looked at me and told me to start a list so I would remember. Don't worry—for the rest of my life, I will work to show my appreciation and pay it forward.

Thank you.

Notes

1. Steve Miller Band, "Fly Like an Eagle," by Steve Miller, recorded 1976 on *Fly Like an Eagle,* Capitol Records.
2. *The Wizard of Oz,* directed by Victor Fleming (1939; Burbank, CA: Warner Home Video, 2014), DVD.
3. Max Lucado, *You Are Special* (Wheaton, IL: Crossway, 1997).
4. Michael Hyatt, *Platform: Getting Noticed in a Noisy World* (Nashville: Thomas Nelson, 2012).
5. Marie Kondo, *The Life-Changing Magic of Tidying Up: The Japanese Art of Decluttering and Organizing* (New York: Ten Speed, 2014).
6. Alli Worthington, *Breaking Busy: How to Find Peace and Purpose in a World of Crazy* (Grand Rapids, MI: Zondervan, 2016).
7. Henry David Thoreau, *Walden: Or Life in the Woods* (CreateSpace, 2014), 51. First published 1854 by Ticknor and Fields (Boston).
8. "Meet Zach Sobiech: My Last Days," SoulPancake, video, 22:20, May 3, 2013, www.youtube.com/watch?v=9NjKgV65fpo.
9. OneRepublic, "Marchin On," by Ryan Tedder, recorded 2009 on *Waking Up,* Interscope Records.
10. Evan Andrews, "9 Things You May Not Know About the Oregon Trail," History.com, November 13, 2015, www.history.com/news /history-lists/9-things-you-may-not-know-about-the-oregon-trail.

About the Author

Rachel Marie Martin believes in life's possibilities. Having pulled herself up from poverty to being named one of *Inc.* magazine's top eighteen up-and-coming women entrepreneurs, Rachel has been writing her blog, *Finding Joy,* full time for several years and writing online for more than a decade. Her articles have been translated into more than twenty-five languages and featured in numerous worldwide publications. She is the author of *Dear Mom Letters* and has been a contributor in numerous other books.

She is passionate about embracing a daring, adventure-filled, "what if" life and is often requested to speak and motivate others using her vivacious energy and deep belief that life is a time-sensitive gift.

Rachel is also a partner in Audience Industries, the world's largest training-and-development company for bloggers, authors, creatives, and entrepreneurs. She travels worldwide teaching marketing, voice, messaging, social media strategy, and goal setting. She is the one who will tell others to "knock it off with the excuses" and then will explain the strategy for getting from point A to point B.

Rachel is a single mom to seven kids: Hannah, Chloé, Grace, Brennan, Caleb, Elijah, and Samuel. She spent most of her years in the frozen tundra of Minnesota but now calls the music city of Nashville, Tennessee, her home.

finding joy

Community. We all want it and we have it.

Just as the women in San Diego didn't let me fall, I don't want you to read this book, start working toward your brave, and then lose that mojo. Instead, take your bravery a step further and join our community of women who don't have time for the masks in life and believe in encouraging and standing shoulder to shoulder with other women.

We'll circle our wagons with you.

Life is too short to walk this process alone.

Share your dream.

Join our conversation at Facebook.com/findingjoyblog.

It's real. Empathetic. Emotional. Mask free. And beyond that, the place to receive daily reminders that keep you moving, keep you motivated, and keep you remembering your heart.

We're waiting for you.

Twitter: @finding_joy
Instagram: @finding_joy
Blog: findingjoy.net
Speaking: findingjoy.net/keynote
Email: info@findingjoy.net